Developing the Architecture of the Workplace: Gensler 1967-1997

Copyright © 1998
by Edizioni Press, Inc.
All rights reserved. No part
of this book may be
reproduced in any form
without written permission
of the copyright owners.
All images in this book
have been reproduced
with the consent of the
artists concerned and no
responsibility is accepted
by producer, publisher or
printer for any
infringments of copyright
or otherwise, arising from
the contents of this
publication. Every effort
has been made to ensure
that credits comply with
information supplied.

First published in the
United States of America
by Edizioni Press, Inc.
469 West 21st Street
New York, New York 10011
Telephone (212) 924-4164
Fax (212) 691-0524

ISBN 0-9662230-0-4

Library of Congress
Catalogue Card Number:
98-70622

Printed in Italy
by Grafiche Mariano

Design and composition:
Libra Associati

Editorial Director:
Pierantonio Giacoppo

Copy Editors:
Meghan Daily
Anat Rosenberg

Front cover:
Epson America, Inc.
Torrance, California
Photograph:
© Marco Lorenzetti,
Hedrich Blessing

Front flap (left to right):
Edward C. Friedrichs,
Margo Grant Walsh,
M. Arthur Gensler Jr. and
Antony Harbour
Photograph:
© Elliott Kaufman

Table of Contents

	Introductions
7	**Know Your Client, Know Your Client's Business** by M. Arthur Gensler Jr., FAIA, FIIDA, RIBA
10	**Workplace Design Through Analysis and the Creation of Standards** by Margo Grant Walsh
18	**Solutions for Dynamic Problems** by Antony Harbour
21	**Designing in an Era of Continual Change** by Edward C. Friedrichs, FAIA, IIDA
26	**Developing the Architecture of the Workplace: Gensler** by Anthony Iannacci
	Projects
32	**Prudential Insurance Company of America, Westlake, Texas**
38	**RepublicBank of Houston, Houston, Texas**
48	**Goldman, Sachs & Company**
50	Goldman, Sachs & Company, New York, New York
56	Goldman, Sachs International Ltd., London
64	**Enron Corp, Houston, Texas**
76	**Union Bank of Switzerland, New York, New York**
80	**Apple Computer, Inc.**
84	Apple Computer, Inc. De Anza 3, Cupertino, California
88	Apple Computer, Inc. Research and Development, Cupertino, California
94	Apple Computer, Inc. U.S. Customer Service Center, Austin, Texas
98	**Becton Dickinson Immunocytometry Systems, San Jose, California**
106	**Epson America, Inc., Torrance, California**
116	**Taylor + Smith, Houston, Texas**
122	**Davis Polk & Wardwell, New York, New York**
128	**HarperCollins Publishers, San Francisco, California**
134	**MCI Communications Corp., Colorado Springs, Colorado**
146	**Morrison & Foerster, Palo Alto, California**
150	**MasterCard International, Purchase, New York**
156	**Chevron Corporation, San Francisco, California**
164	**Hoffmann-La Roche, Inc., Nutley, New Jersey**
170	**Board of Governors of the Federal Reserve System, Board Room, Washington, D.C.**
174	**Columbia/HCA Call Center, Bedford, Texas**
178	**Netscape Communications, Mountain View and Sunnyvale, California**
186	**Workplace Task Force**
196	Credits

Know Your Client, Know Your Client's Business

by M. Arthur Gensler Jr.,
FAIA, FIIDA, RIBA

If I were asked what I consider the most important directive in Gensler's workplace design, it would be "Know your client and know your client's business." As architects of ideas and architects of solutions, our passion is to create work environments that facilitate the client's business process and support efficient, cost-effective delivery of their goods and services. To accomplish this mission, I urge Gensler team members to first educate themselves about, and intensively interact with, not only the client, but also all the other participants in the client's operation.

As an avid observer of the business world, I see companies today being bombarded with change on numerous fronts: organizational restructuring, demographic concerns, technological innovation, environmental and health issues, and economic fluctuation. The spirit of change is permeating business, and for me, change is not a simple, one-time event, but an ongoing journey. In order to stay competitive, companies are restructuring themselves to be more dynamic, more innovative, more flexible and, most importantly, to be agile.

The concept of agility represents a new way of understanding our corporate clients and their relationships to the public and the business arena. Focused on creating products or delivering services as rapidly and as cost-effectively as possible, today's agile company is forging strategic long-term relationships and alliances with consultants, suppliers, customers and even competitors. No longer a collection of separate functions pulling in various directions, the company's team must be an integrated whole, a strong link in an even stronger chain of players. Companies are realizing the advantages of structuring themselves into cross-functional teams, rethinking their business processes and operating as virtual companies. As a designer, I am challenged by the need to move

Consolidated Freightways, Palo Alto, CA
This simple and straightforward 1982 Gensler interior design solution expresses the client's corporate image, serves the end-user's environmental well-being, and supports the architectural intent.

DMB&B, Troy, MI
For the 1996 relocation of its offices, advertising giant DMB&B was ready to change its surroundings to support a new style of work and a new image. Gensler developed a flexible planning approach that allows DMB&B to reorganize teams without making significant changes to either the architecture or the workstations. All members of each brand team are clustered together for enhanced collaboration.

ahead of all these forces of change in order to respond quickly and appropriately to our customers' facility needs.

The dynamic of workplace design is undergoing transformation, a process that really began in the early 1980s when we saw the debunking of many of the basic tenets that guided the way a business operated. Companies are moving away from basing production runs solely on market predictions; instead they are looking directly to their specific customer base as the best indicator for their course of action. Companies are focusing less on the product and more on the customer, and by tapping into the many new technologies, they can address the specific needs of a large variety of customers. The key issue is time; companies want to know how different methods of working, management strategies, and space planning will affect the time it takes them to respond to their client's needs or to bring a product or service to the market. The organization of an agile company allows it to thrive on this change and uncertainty, and its structure (including the workplace) must be flexible enough to permit rapid reconfiguration of both people and space keyed to the needs of different customers.

Today, nothing is a given. I am proud that one of our most important recent accomplishments was to develop a variety of tools to help Gensler clients get the work environments they need. These services include: Strategic Facilities Planning, which helps a company to determine long-range operational plans and corresponding facility needs; Universal Planning, which allows companies to move people without moving walls or workstations; Gensler Information Solutions, which tracks square footages and people and provides charge-back information; and Facilities Management, which helps companies manage the process after the initial installation. By developing and implementing workplace standards and a kit-of-parts approach, we can provide clients with maximum flexibility with a minimum of disruption.

One area in which I strongly encourage our growing involvement is the consolidation and tracking of real estate assets when two companies merge or an acquisition is made. We are able to help organizations determine maximum space utilization and help them plan for the management of their real estate assets. This process becomes even more critical when two organizations with overlapping markets merge, creating more complex moves, renovation, and/or disposition of assets. One of our more challenging assignments is to develop a merger and acquisition plan for the real estate that is based on the organization's customer, staffing, operations, and geographic requirements. This plan is often complicated by many sequential factors; it must reflect requirements from combined business units, telecommunications and information systems, as well as spatial limitations imposed by existing facilities, laws, building codes, ownerships, and leases.

How does all of this change, corporate restructuring, and repositioning affect the workplace? For one thing, companies are realizing that cutting costs, through downsizing or consolidation, will not necessarily make them more competitive. Success comes from using all available resources - time, people, money, information, technology, organizational structure, and space - to their fullest potential. It is very satisfying that our workplace design can, in very substantial ways, enhance a company's physical and human resources.

Statistics show that the workforce has increased, but there remains a high office vacancy rate in many cities; where did all the people go? They chose other options. The virtual office is here, as is hotelling, where employees call ahead to reserve office

Bank of America, Pasadena, CA
A recent project for a client who has worked with Gensler since 1970 in locations all over world. Providing the variety of design services that Bank of America requires in each project, Gensler assembles the teams from around the Gensler firm.

BankBoston, Boston, MA
A major component of Gensler's work in the late 90s is helping companies through the merger and acquisition process by tracking, evaluating, and planning combined work space from the two companies. Gensler planned BankBoston's headquarters and provided program management of various facilities during their merger with Shawmut Bank.

space for a specific time frame, similar to making hotel reservations, and telecommuting, where staff members work primarily from a remote location, usually their home, and are linked to their companies by telephone, modem, and personal computer. Companies like IBM and AT&T, who place a high premium on customer contact, use hotelling or telecommuting offices for some of their employees. I take the somewhat controversial position that alternative office programs, while becoming more common, will ultimately be only a small portion of the total work environment. However, designers must still address the issue of educating users of alternative office space of the purpose and appropriate use of an unfamiliar environment.

Another key role a design firm plays in creating the workplace is to manage the multiple components and activities that make up a project. We must ensure not only that the planning is correct and that the occupants know how to use the space, but also that the lighting and circuitry are appropriate, the air quality is maximized and efficient, that the proper cabling and technology are in place, and that the build-out construction is environmentally sensitive.

Having practiced the architecture of the workplace for more than four decades, I truly believe that workplace design will not diminish as an area of practice. With the inevitability of escalating office rents, companies will always demand efficient and flexible office space to meet changing operational needs. At Gensler, we will continue, as we have done for over three decades, to assist building owners in developing appropriate building configurations and interior standards and systems. I never tire of relating to our staff and to clients the fact that in 1965 we began as a three-person office in San Francisco, planning interior spaces for the Alcoa Building, a speculative project. At that point, our sole mission was to help tenants determine how much space they needed, how it should be used, and how the interior must suit their individual needs and present the image that they, the client, not the designer, wanted. To me, the most important part of Gensler's story is that we are still listening to our customers, learning all about them, and leading them where they didn't know they wanted to go. Together, we stretch our imaginations to create a unique workplace.

In looking through the following project presentations, you will see that there is no "Gensler look or solution," but you will be able to see the quality of design and planning that we work hard to uphold in all our projects. All of us on the Gensler team agree that our job is to reflect the image and operation of a particular company, especially in working with an organization to create a work environment. I find myself and my co-workers spending more and more time interacting with the business community, and attending a wide range of meetings and seminars to try to understand our clients' needs and what's appropriate for them in that city, that site, that business. When a client commissioned Frank Lloyd Wright, the look and the image were Wright's, and the client made the value judgment that that was what was wanted. When a client approaches Gensler, I firmly believe that it's with the trust that we will create an environment that is right for that company, its clients and employees, that the space will be professionally done, well thought out, controlled in time and budget, and have lasting value. Our goal is not to have people say, "That's a Gensler job." We would like them to say, "This is a terrific facility; who did it?" We know that in order to stay competitive, we must keep our customers competitive; by helping them to succeed in their business, we will succeed in ours.

Gensler San Francisco office
Typical workstation area with glass-fronted conference room. Visual communication and informal gathering places are emphasized in the award-winning office.

Gensler Washington, D.C. office
The main focus of the plan and design is on creating the most appropriate workplace to support cooperation and innovation.

Workplace Design Through Analysis and the Creation of Standards

by Margo Grant Walsh

As designers of the workplace, I believe ours is a cyclical route rather than a linear path forward. The business world does not so much evolve as it reinvents, re-engineers and reorganizes itself in a different configuration, adapts itself to the current economic environment, and begins the cycle again. I believe there has been no dramatic, fundamental change in the workplace over the past forty years, merely variations and permutations of existing conditions. Customer contact was once primarily face-to-face and one-on-one, but today it takes place through the technology of the Internet, the telephone, and fax machines. Where production was once dependent on the typewriter, now every worker has access to a computer. Where we once specified desks, we now specify workstations. Where we once dictated documents, we now prepare our own. Where work was once performed "at the office," offices are now everywhere. We can use our cellular phone at the airport and on the plane, our carphone while in transit, our laptops wherever we wish. While the need for the "home base" is still essential, in effect we may have five or six "workplaces" as opposed to the one "home base." In effect, we are always working.

I began my career in the work environment in 1954 with the U.S. National Bank in Portland, Oregon. During my three years working in the bank, I became well acquainted with the way employees, managers, and customers interact. During my early years with the bank, we (including the President and Chief Executive) worked in an open plan environment, resulting in easy interpersonal interaction and communication. In 1960, I started my career as a designer in an architectural office and sat in a large drafting room, where everyone could see everyone else. We shared telephones; we all had the same type of drafting table, and by strolling through the office and looking over shoulders you

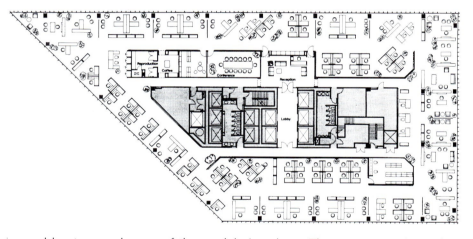

Pennzoil Company, Houston, TX
Pennzoil Company, Gensler's first major corporate headquarters project, is located in a pair of 36-story trapezoidal black towers (designed by Philip Johnson) that mirror each other on a city block in downtown Houston. This plan demonstrates a unique planning configuration that is identical in elevation and in section.

could get a good sense of the work being done. There was no privacy, but a tremendous quality of communication, high productivity, and a strong staff interaction outside the work environment. In 1997, the emphasis is now on privacy for the worker, with spaces planned for "teaming" (whether or not effective teaming really does take place in those areas). As everyone works on computers, in some businesses and professions it is sometimes difficult to measure what and how employees are doing.

The determining factor of 75 percent of today's design and planning work is not increasing productivity or enhancing interaction, but saving real estate costs and ideally, creating more flexibility in the work environment, and reducing the cost of churn and change. Since statements regarding the increase of productivity have been extremely hard to quantify, few concrete examples exist. Technology, not necessarily innovative thinking or delineation of hierarchy, is the driving force behind much of the design of the workplace. It is my belief that although technology often requires less manpower, it may often result in less effective customer service. Where a customer once could request and receive a printout of a bank statement in twenty-four hours and have direct, personal contact with a customer service representative (the statement clerk), it now requires passing through layers of workers, complex and sometimes confusing and lengthy voice instructions, and more time to process the request.

A key issue in the workplace is flexibility, which is intrinsically tied to technology. Innovation in workplace design is likewise linked to the state of available technology. The Quickborner Group, influential and early innovators in workplace design in the 1960s, may have gone farther faster if they had not been so limited by the integration of technology into furniture systems. The Weyerhaeuser installation was one of the first examples of a furniture manufacturer's responding to the need for an appropriate open plan furniture product. However, by 1970, the rapid advance of technology (and its wiring "tail") had significantly affected the visual order of space, not to mention the increase in heat load on the environment due to the cathode ray tube.

Technology is currently causing a redistribution of space rather than a reduction of space. For instance, the job of a multi-task, professional secretary/administrative assistant is changing in scope; even the term "secretary" (from the Latin word secretum for secret) is now politically incorrect. The secretarial (assistant) work space is growing in size and efficiency to accommodate fax machines, printers, more document handling, convenient files, mail for multiple managers, and oversized mailing box storage. Essentials such as printers and fax machines are often shared by assistants clustered in pairs or small teams. Thus, as private offices have seen a downward trend in size, open plan assistant workstations have held or increased their square footage. In addition, today's technologically confident workers have less need for the production capabilities of a secretary, instead producing, editing, and copying their own documents.

Today, designing the workplace is not just about planning space or identifying the appropriate workstation footprint; it involves a thorough investigation of what a building can offer, including how its electrical and mechanical systems can support the firm's technology requirements. The new dimensions to all this are the recent myriad issues surrounding ergonomics, sustainable design and sick building syndrome, handicapped access, life safety codes, etc. We have to be as cognizant of, and responsive to, such environmental and physical concerns as fumes from equipment, carpal tunnel syndrome, and other problems as we are to module, floorplate and adjacency issues.

Pennzoil Company, Houston, TX
In its new headquarters (1976), Pennzoil sought a single, cohesive corporate environment that would integrate employees being relocated from several locations. Gensler's task: create a unified culture and achieve efficiency by eliminating redundancy inherent in the multiple business locations.

In addition to technological, environmental and code issues, financial factors significantly influence a company's facility options. There are three important factors that influence a real estate decision: cultural acceptability, location acceptability, and financial acceptability. The financial issue will ultimately drive the decision, followed by the right location. Culture can be adjusted to suit the other two factors.

This theory can be dramatically seen in corporate America, which enjoyed very generous facility budgets in the 1960s through the early 1980s. Workers believed that status entitled them to an office equipped with a level of furniture and finishes that corresponded to their job title and responsibility. As hierarchy became more and more important, we found it necessary to develop multiple standards. "If your name is on the door, there is a Bigelow on the floor" was more often true than not. The leaner 1990s have produced reduction in personnel in some businesses, and virtually eliminated multiple space standards, which used to be assigned by hierarchy, with a wide range of office sizes for a variety of positions. Now, it is common to have a large corporation utilize only two different office sizes for the majority of the staff, with only very senior executives given larger work spaces and one or two open plan space standards for other personnel.

The projects selected for feature presentation in this book are representative of the different types of projects for which we are recognized. These projects demonstrate how we work with clients in new and proposed buildings, retrofits of older structures, and on suburban corporate campuses to create functional work spaces as real estate markets and business conditions shift. We find that some firms involve their young professionals in the design process, and these potential leaders have strong opinions about financial commitment, image, flexibility, and technology. We also find corporations involving spokesmen for the staff in facility task forces and planning groups. These firms approach their facility design with the same level of thoughtful questioning and precision they bring to their business and professional assignments.

In 1972, Pennzoil Company made the decision to consolidate its business units from disparate sites to a new landmark headquarters in a pair of 36-story trapezoidal black towers (designed by Philip Johnson) that mirror each other on a 2.3-acre city block in downtown Houston. In the oil business, Pennzoil is known in the industry for quality and fighting tenacity. The image it wanted to project, both internally and externally, was "more than a yellow oil can." Throughout the headquarters, the client sought a single, cohesive corporate image capable of unifying employees from seven Houston locations and offices in Shreveport, Louisiana, who were being consolidated in this entirely new corporate environment. Gensler executed all interior spaces in the entire North Tower, to be occupied by Pennzoil Company and its former subsidiary, United Gas Pipe Line Company.

Gensler's task was twofold: create a unified corporate culture, and achieve efficiency by eliminating the redundancy inherent in the multiple business locations. By the time the client moved in, Gensler had performed services ranging from assistance with base building systems evaluations to lease negotiations and move-in coordination and occupancy, as well as interior design.

One basic decision by Pennzoil management was to incorporate an open planning system in order to accommodate subsequent changes without major demolition or reconstruction expense. Only executives and the exploration staff stayed in private offices. This open planning approach defined the need for a system of workstations

Mobil Oil Corporation, Fairfax, VA (left)
The Mobil offices are a strong demonstration of the importance of having an appropriate building module.

Mobil Oil Corporation, Fairfax, VA (right)
Supervisor's office within open plan follows workstation and square footage standards that were established for all employee levels.

suitable for both middle management and clerical staff. Since existing panel systems did not have wiring capabilities and substance present in today's products, Gensler specified a Stow Davis case goods system for both the uniformity offered and the efficiency of limited options. The open plan workstations also facilitated communication. Having the case good systems, the freestanding office furniture, was a way to visually provide a more permanent sense to the internal environment. Tempered glass panels were also used to divide semi-private offices and introduce further visual interest.

Pennzoil also requested that each floor be executed in varied color schemes to avoid a feeling of sameness while minimizing inventory and relocation problems. The reception area on each floor incorporates a visual element representing the specific business unit housed on that floor, another design device to emphasize Pennzoil's importance in the business community. Variety was achieved through the creation of twenty separate color schemes based on five carpet colors, two wood finishes, and a large number of fabrics in solids and prints. The varied colors, textures, and finishes, with glass dividers and dramatic photomurals, provide natural definition of the work areas.

The Pennzoil project, which lasted four and one half years, includes virtually all elements of corporate headquarters planning and typifies the multiple steps necessary to create modern office facilities for a growing organization. Pennzoil was Gensler's first major corporate headquarters project, and it raised the level of quality and permanence we bring to our clients' facilities. On a recent tour of Pennzoil, I discovered just how classic our design and planning efforts were for this client; much of the facility exists just as it was planned, over two decades ago. Interestingly enough, the sloped ceilings (produced by the trapezoidal building form) were the real challenge in design, and efficient office usage remains a problem. All of the offices that were created in this space remain, but many of the open plan workstations that were provided are empty. Given the choice, people have migrated to the privacy of the office.

Our success with Pennzoil led to our being hired by Mobil to create their new headquarters. In 1997, Gensler Houston embarked on the restack and reevaluation of this building. For the new Mobil Oil headquarters in Fairfax, Virginia, we were asked to create a master concept to significantly reduce the time needed to accommodate change. Developed at the height of the "open plan" furniture/space solution, the new headquarters building was designed to be 100 percent open plan when, in fact, Mobil had very rigid standards that, when finally established, actually required 65 percent closed offices and 35 percent open workstations. The building was under construction when we were brought on. We therefore had to take a building designed for open plan, address Mobil's programmatic needs, and come up with an innovative way to use the building. Since the mechanical cores, stairs, and toilets were situated at the ends of the building, we decided to leave open the center of the floorplate and create three well-defined circulation systems that thread their way throughout the general work floors and give unity to the "open band" concept we established. Essential to the success of the project was maintaining workstation and square footage standards for all employee levels, resulting in four workstation types for the open band area and three managerial office types. A critical aspect of the planning was to bring daylight into the work space and allow all employees to have access to the beautiful rural Virginia setting.

The senior executive directing the project for Mobil said that the government would never come to business, so business must go to government, hence the move from New

Mobil Oil Corporation, Fairfax, VA
Three well defined circulation systems thread their way throughout the general work floors and give unity to the open band concept established by Gensler.

York City to Fairfax. Gensler had to sell the design to employees, who were being asked to move out of New York and adapt culturally and psychologically to the new environment. Our dilemma was how to make the new facility attractive, while asking most of the workers to move from a private office to an open plan environment. We presented a detailed scale model of the facility, as well as a full-scale office and furniture mockup, to employees in sixty "marketing" sessions. We began with the relocation of Mobil's Marketing and Refining Division; today the majority of staff is situated in Fairfax.

The Mobil assignment was the impetus for opening Gensler New York. It was one of the first times we led a team of other design consultants (who had special areas of expertise and a long-term relationship with the executives at Mobil), and integrated their efforts with our own assignment. We developed a cohesiveness among the groups, each with its own different personality. While the Mobil interiors are extremely functional and highly flexible, fine materials and detailing created a professional corporate image and an airy, unencumbered work environment.

My experience in designing workplaces for major corporations such as Pennzoil and Mobil, as well as for other financial, legal and professional service firms, has reinforced my belief that the planning module is a critical factor in efficient interior space use. It is the common denominator for all office sizes and planning concepts. The best office module for each client is the module that is best suited to office requirements, provides good interior circulation, is compatible with efficient open plan furniture systems for administrative and support personnel, and is easy to work with in the construction of doors, partitioning, and other interior components.

The building core design is another variable that strongly affects the organization of interior space. The core (which contains elevators, stairs, restrooms, and mechanical, electrical, and service facilities) is a basic element in the highly efficient use of office space. Ideally, the core should be the smallest size possible, while still effectively accommodating the necessary functions. The ideal floorplate shape and module vary from client to client, since the company's operations and culture ultimately dictate the most appropriate plan. To arrive at the most suitable floorplate, the interior architect will analyze the client's workflow patterns, optimum departmental adjacencies, privacy and status considerations, and space and furniture standards. The ultimate lesson to be learned from the study of floorplate issues is that every building can be maximized by sound planning and design strategies. With grit, determination, and ingenuity, a good designer can make any building work; however, some work environments will be more efficient than others.

Because of Gensler's wide range of experience in all building types, we intuitively know when looking at a floorplate whether it will accommodate the client's needs. Addressing the client's growing concern for efficient utilization of space, Gensler's New York office began performing detailed benchmarking analyses on how representative clients - major law firms, insurance companies, financial institutions, and investment banks - use space. The initial focus of the research has been on law firms and financial institutions, which we classify by size and headquarters location. This benchmarking process enables our clients to get an accurate, statistically based view of how comparable business types (which are not identified by name) are allocating office space.

Overall, our law offices and financial institutions benchmarking studies have shown that there is a tremendous consistency of space use percentages among firms that are

Wachtell, Lipton, Rosen & Katz, New York, NY
In creating the law office for this major New York law firm, Gensler focused much attention on the main conference area that contains reconfigurable tables and many seating options to accommodate a wide variety of client and staff meetings.

Wachtell, Lipton, Rosen & Katz, New York, NY
Secretarial quads, located at the corners of the floor plan, serve to break open the corridors and increase operational efficiency by allowing secretaries to work as teams.

similar in size and region, regardless of the building footprint. The sizes of the various offices are not always driven by the individual floorplate, but often by how the primary circulation is allocated. The less space dedicated to circulation, the more space that can be allocated to the workplace. One of the most critical factors in developing successful space utilization is an efficiently planned circulation factor, which can be as low as 20 percent or as high as 35 percent, depending on the building footprint, layout, planning depths, location and configuration of the building core.

Our benchmarking process raises design above the intuitive level. It helps to speed up the planning process by expediting space planning decisions, and gives clients confidence, knowing what comparable firms are achieving in their space utilization in terms of fact-based, yet confidential, information. The analysis creates an economic model for design services that may profoundly alter the traditional relationship of designer and client by helping the public to measure the quality of what we do.

Since much of our initial benchmarking work has focused on law offices, we can make some general observations about this area of workplace design. Perhaps nowhere has technology had more of an impact than in the law library, which is not the focal point it used to be. With firms putting volumes in condensed storage systems and libraries assuming less prominence overall, less space is being dedicated to books. The library may be deemed almost obsolete, but our practical experience to date is that it is hard for senior lawyers to give up their books as reference. We are in a transition period where the technologies and services that obviate the need for books are still being developed and defined.

If the library has lost its place as the focal point in today's typical law firm, that role has been assumed by the conference center. The development of the centralized conference area has been the result of both technological know-how and the pressing need to control costs. Firms want the ability to conduct teleconferencing and service full-day meetings, as well as to provide food service during these meetings. Today's conference centers usually include a series of flexibly sized meeting rooms, caucus rooms, food service, and an adjacent support services department. For the law firm of Shearman & Sterling, we developed a major conference center, with eleven-foot ceilings, three large conference rooms, four smaller spaces, five caucus rooms and facilities for word processing and faxing.

The amount of space dedicated to reception is also changing. More firms are locating a reception area on every second or third floor, rather than on every level. Clients are greeted on the nearest reception floor, and floors with no reception areas have security doors and telephones for access.

For Wachtell, Lipton, Rosen & Katz, the ability to respond to changes in personnel and space needs was a key priority. Gensler was able to design enough flexibility into the plan of their new space in New York's CBS Building ("Black Rock") to temporarily house some of the "interior" personnel, such as paralegals, in future associate offices. The 23,000-square-foot floorplate has many advantages, including a five-foot planning module, which allows uniform partner offices and associate offices. The unusual "core within a core" design permits support areas to abut the core with no secondary circulation loop. On the non-reception floors, small storage rooms are included for potential conversion to additional reception areas. Every interior support space has been pre-wired for future use as a private office and every associate office can be doubled. The major conference area

Goldman Sachs International Limited, London
Because the nature of doing business in London involves more client meetings, having sufficient conference areas and client meeting rooms was important for Goldman Sachs International Limited.

Cravath, Swaine & Moore, NY
To accommodate employees' needs for last-minute child care, Cravath, Swaine & Moore worked with Gensler to create the first emergency child care center for a New York law firm.

contains reconfigurable tables and many seating options. Additional flexibility was permitted with the option of taking another floor in the near future or, conversely, of eliminating the lowest floor of the stack with no loss of essential support functions.

The support floors, located in the mid-stack, were carefully planned in the sequence of the workflow, from document creation, to reproduction, and mailroom. The corridors are treated like streets with "shop windows" open to the various departments to avoid unnecessary traffic and disruption of work within. Secretarial quads, located at the corners of the floor plan, serve to break open the corridors, accommodate required adjacencies to attorney offices, organize the files, centralize supplies, provide shared equipment, and increase operational efficiency by working as teams. The design also includes a seven-story interconnecting stair with atrium and two main reception areas positioned to serve two half-floor conference centers. The new office environment created by Gensler for Wachtell, Lipton, Rosen & Katz is a strong example of how an important architectural landmark can, with the proper planning and design, accommodate a world-class professional firm. We are presently doing additional planning for this firm.

In planning the Cravath, Swaine & Moore space in New York's World Financial Center, we urged the partners to rethink their planning concept. We suggested that intermingling support functions with attorneys on every floor should give way to a new stacking plan dedicating two of the thirteen floors to support functions, nine floors to attorneys, and the remaining floors to the conference center, law library and cafeteria. It was a whole new mind-set for Cravath. Windows, normally reserved for private offices, were provided for open plan work areas on support floors, and in the records center. One of the innovations incorporated into the facility is an emergency child care center, which at the time was the only one available in a New York law firm. The space is planned to be very open so that children can be easily watched by the small staff in the child care center.

Financial firms have many of the same space requirements as law firms, with the added need for areas dedicated to trading, trading support and larger operations and technology. Many of our projects in the past three years have involved consolidating business operations and assisting financial institutions and corporations in identifying creative ways to use space. In financial firms and investment banks, status and flexibility continue to be an important consideration since in a very competitive market status (personalization, office sizes, and sometimes views) can be important. These organizations also want the hard facts yielded by benchmarking studies. Gensler recognizes that the costs of real estate and personnel must be controlled. The impact of technology and the ability to build systems that support it are critical.

Established by J. Pierpont Morgan in New York in 1861, JP Morgan & Co. has financed many of the enterprises - railroads, steel, mining, and utilities - that established the United States as a modern industrial power. Most of those early clients still maintain relationships with Morgan today, as do a wide variety of new companies, which rely on the firm for a full range of integrated capabilities, which include capital raising, strategic advice, market access, and asset management. Our association with JP Morgan began in 1985, when we were retained to program and design their new headquarters planned at 60 Wall Street (designed by Kevin Roche, John Dinkeloo and Associates) on a large mid-block site in the heart of the financial district. JP Morgan purchased the 1.6 million

Gensler New York office
The New York office provides numerous conference rooms of various sizes as well as large spaces for entertaining and hosting all staff events.

MasterCard International, Purchase, NY
For its world headquarters, MasterCard International chose an I.M. Pei-designed building, which offers large floor areas on each level and a simple horizontal organization. Gensler's challenge was to accommodate the evolving operation of a world-class

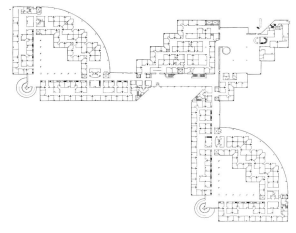

square-foot tower from George Klein/Park Tower Realty at 60 Wall Street. Based on our winning design competition entry, JP Morgan surveyed the building and asked us to create their new headquarters space. While plans for the building shell had already been approved, we were able to modify the module to accommodate required building components and workstation standards. While we did not do intensive individual programming, we did take the existing program and worked with projections given to us by the bank's real estate and facilities group. Throughout the project, we were mindful of the basic tenets of the bank's culture - integrity, objectivity, and judgment.

Since JP Morgan cultivates a "family" philosophy among employees, one of our team's major tasks was focusing on the individual's functional space. The forty office floors are based on a generic planning concept where conference pods are always sited in the same location and the 3,000 plus workstations have identical footprints. The number of adjacent private offices and flexible work rooms vary according to floor function, and since the conference pod is the only permanently enclosed space on the floor, it also serves as the design element. We extended corridors to the core in order to accommodate copy rooms, equipment spaces, etc., and incorporated raised flooring throughout the office. The generic space plan we created for that facility has enabled the bank to control its churn costs and to increase operational flexibility. At the time the JP Morgan 60 Wall Street facility was the largest New York project for which we used three-dimensional computer generated studies as important design tools. Because of JP Morgan's requirement for cost effectiveness, and ease and flexibility of maintenance, very few colors were selected, and acoustical and lighting elements were carefully chosen. Sensitive to ecological and safety matters, JP Morgan demanded non-toxic materials and even though handicapped codes had not been initiated, we specified all-lever hardware.

The second project for JP Morgan was to house the Investment Group in a 1960s building that was once a hotel with an office tower added-on. Again, we were given the assignment based on winning a design competition. We performed very thorough programming of business units in order to locate them in the small footprint with numerous private offices. While evaluating other buildings, we continued to look at stay-in-place scenarios, since we learned from staff interviews that their 522 Fifth Avenue location had been home to them for many years, and its proximity to Grand Central Station and many midtown clubs and services was a significant advantage.

The 522 Fifth Avenue planning concept, which is a further evolution of the thinking and development that began at 60 Wall Street, utilizes a universal footprint and develops office sizes with an emphasis on flexibility. The building is a wedding cake configuration (floor sizes diminish towards the top of the building) and we installed an interconnecting stair to enhance internal communication. There is one basic workstation size and the furniture is made of a lighter wood, is more architectural, more refined and provides more privacy. Installing raised flooring presented a challenge in the older building, since we had to determine where to put in ramping so that it would not affect space usage and provide the connection from slab to raised floors. As a result of our work on these projects, we continue to serve the bank in numerous restacking, replanning, and "box" move efforts.

During my design career, I have worked intensively with law firms, financial institutions, and major corporations. I have developed a knowledge of how these professions operate. As the practice of business evolves, so do the considerations and criteria for designing appropriate work environments. As designers, we have to be ahead of the cycle. We have to know where business is heading and think about business operation the way the client thinks. Our job is to respect the intelligence and flow of the business world, provide thoughtful and appropriate design and planning services, and create work environments that allow employees, management, and customers to interact in the most positive, productive way. At any one point in time, all businesses are concerned with achieving the greatest density with the most efficiency, comfort, and flexibility. When we begin the process for each new workplace project, we must bring to it all our experience, ingenuity, and resourcefulness. Anything less will not be enough. The process of developing a facility is always challenging, but keeping clients happy means to continue to work with them after occupancy to help them maximize the value of what we designed, and to adapt to the changing business world.

Solutions for Dynamic Problems

by Antony Harbour

I believe that good design is one of the most valuable resources available to a business. I approach projects with an enthusiasm that is based on the realization that good design provides innovative solutions, attracts the best people, sells products, and adds value to the company. As the visual signature of a company, the influence of design is pervasive. We have found that our designs are able to both mirror and project corporate strategies, and have played an integral part in shaping those strategies. By communicating the company's respect for its employees, we believe that our designs stimulate their best efforts.

Design for me represents the process of generating planning solutions to what are essentially dynamic problems - people, relationships, work flow, communication. I know we have created good interior design when the result is a space that is organized and equipped for the work people do. It must be practical, efficient, dynamic, personal, functional, and flexible. As an architect of the workplace, my role is to help clients achieve their goals through design. One of the aspects of interior design that I enjoy most is helping clients look at a building from the inside out, to help them understand if the building will really work for them. It is through this early analysis that we are able to increase the efficiency of the leased space or, in the case of a major tenant, to increase the efficiency of the proposed building before its final design. Our design work carries us through every detail of the facility, not simply the finishes, furniture, and fabrics on the executive floors, but the vistas and light sources for employees in offices, work stations, and computer areas as well. Our work carries us into spaces as diversified as private dining rooms and health facilities, and to aspects of corporate identity, signage, and graphics. All of this is part of the process

Baker & Botts, Dallas, TX
Gensler's challenge in designing this Dallas law office was to unify all floors in a coherent extension of a design scheme and standards Gensler previously developed for other Baker & Botts offices. By continuing the design into all areas of the space, Gensler was able to create a unified and workable environment.

Society Bank Cafeteria, Cleveland, OH
As companies focus on the most economical and efficient space planning, employee amenities are taking on increasing importance. In Society Bank's headquarters, the celebratory cafeteria space features a 50-foot-high skylight highlighted by a colorful canopy and palm trees.

of creating interiors, and from my perspective it is all client-driven.

In discussing effective workplace design with my team members, there appears to be a consensus that the most fundamental criteria is flexibility, flexibility to reconfigure work teams, to incorporate or remove subsidiary groups as companies merge or spinoff, and in general to adapt the facility to conform to a company's aggressive churn rate. Flexibility is most easily accommodated by standardization. We are seeing an increasing number of companies who work within a diminishing number of standards for workstations, finishes, office sizes, etc. I strongly believe that the process of standardization can become a vehicle for supporting the aesthetic component, not restricting it. Incorporating standards within workplace design and planning provides opportunities for enhancing a space through color, form, and materials as well as accommodating equipment and systems. Standardization sets the stage for an environment of simplicity, strong forms, and clarity, where employees' personalization of space adds to the ambiance of structure rather than contributing to a feeling of chaos.

We began to address this need for standardization in the early 1980s, and I consider the interior design of Allied Bank Plaza in Houston to be one of our landmark projects. One of our biggest challenges was the building itself: a seventy two-story tower encompassing 1.8 million square feet with a footprint composed of symmetrical curves linked by planes, creating the illusion of an ellipse.

During the programming phase, we discovered that many employees, from the CEO to junior executives, were all involved with the same task - lending money. In terms of function, they all could inhabit the same space. Therefore we incorporated a universal office planning system, which was developed especially for this project, a concept that completely reversed prevailing facility management practices by establishing non-hierarchical values in the corporate structure. Executive offices, identical in size, were set along the perimeter and responded to the unusual combination of planes and curves of the building geometry. As departments grew and offices re-assigned, full-height partitions remained intact and office sizes remained constant. In this way, people, rather than spaces were re-arranged.

Another benefit of standardization in the Allied Bank headquarters is that the permanence of the partitions allowed exceptionally fine detailing: brass beading on wood surfaces, custom veneers, and narrow glass reveals that separate the perimeter granite wall from wood partitioning. I recall the Allied Bank design as an instance where the universal office system met the needs of a rapidly growing organization and projected a refined corporate statement.

Since the Allied Bank project, I have utilized the universal planning concept in a variety of projects to standardize the design layout for offices, workstations, and support space locations that are repeated on typical floors. I base universal planning on three principles: move people rather than walls; eliminate physical departments (partitions); and maximize the use of space through interior planning. Once we decide to use the universal plan in a workplace, locations or massings of enclosed spaces are determined based on view, circulation, architecture and growth/reduction options. Open plan workstations are developed as a module or cluster that can be reconfigured by merely switching interior components without re-cabling for electrical outlets and computers. These workstation modules relate to both the space standards and the planning depths to maximize floorplate efficiency.

By repeating the planning concept on typical floors, the client gains flexibility for project teams, departments or entire divisions that can relocate with minimal construction. In an age when change is constant, I have found this to be a highly critical issue: we have learned that it is always more cost-effective to move people than walls.

Rarely do workers' floors compete equally with executive quarters in innovation and design. With the Enron Corp headquarters project, completed in 1989 in Houston, we created an environment that provides a textbook example of how to break down corporate hierarchical barriers through universal planning. Hailed as "a celebration of interior details, a concentration of interior aesthetics and a mastery of interior technology," our work for Enron was the largest interiors project ever created in Houston. It quickly became a national landmark of corporate design for our treatment of the general office floor. The project also became a symbol of the new Houston, where space research, the world's largest medical complex, and a commitment to the arts created a new economic mix for the city which was feeling the effects of the waning oil boom.

In the late 1980s, corporations, and Enron in particular, were learning the benefits of bringing new standards to employees' work environments rather than competing for the most opulent executive floors. Enron is one of the finest examples of how the universal planning concept was able to accommodate the changing needs of a rapidly growing and evolving company. On the forty-six typical floors, a minimum of three private offices are located on the building ends and each floor has a similar flipped symmetrical layout potential for positioning private offices and workstations.

While standardization and universal planning continue to be important concepts of workplace design, other components, such as the use of color or design intervention in employee spaces, are also effective tools. While I was Managing Principal of Gensler Houston, we were involved with a number of limited budget projects that were recognized for their aesthetic and functional value. For our first important project after Enron, the IBM Corporation offices at Two Riverway, we were faced with another unusually shaped building. We redesigned the space planning to optimize adjacencies and to provide outside views for all employees. Low workstations were clustered adjacent to the window walls, while private offices were grouped in the surrounding corners. Not only does this arrangement provide more employees with better views of the surrounding landscape, but it also substantially increases the efficient utilization of space.

Color was another important aspect of the IBM project. We divided the space with strongly proportioned wood partitions finished in bright aniline-dyed veneers, changing from red to blue to green on different floors. We also used a red partition and red elements that relate to the core, the area where the elevators and services are located, to help orient employees. I consider the entire space, which is punctuated by brilliant yellow openings, to be successful from both functional and aesthetic perspectives.

Around the same time, we also utilized the universal planning concept in relocating Houston's Metropolitan Transit Authority to a headquarters facility that would reinforce their new image as one of the country's prime transportation services. Metro required many small private offices and only a few open workstations, so standardized work spaces worked well. However, the long, unbroken corridors presented a hazard of monotony and disorientation. Design time was to be compressed to three and one-half months. Moreover, the budget for renovation was frugal, and the new space was to project a conservative yet progressive image. Not a group to be defeated by the project's challenges, we overcame the problems with the long corridors by transforming them into metaphoric "roads," emphasizing the mass transit identity. The main corridor was widened to represent a major avenue, while cross corridors were narrowed to represent secondary streets. We interrupted the corridors at intervals with workstations or tiled walls in red, yellow or blue; the color indicating the corridor orientation.

At the Dallas offices of the law firm of Baker & Botts, our assignment was to unify all floors through a coherent extension of design standards we had devised for two other branch offices. However, in this project we developed, not just planned, the interiors of both partner and associate offices. By continuing our design into all areas of the space, we were able to create a unified and workable environment.

The last project I would like to cite as an example of our innovative role as workplace designers is the headquarters of Society National Bank, a signature facility in Cleveland, Ohio. Again, the design utilized universal planning on the typical floors. What makes this project unique is how we complemented the standardized floors with very special public spaces. We added amenities to compensate for limiting the number of private offices.

Capital Bank, Miami, FL
This award-winning design established a distinctive presence for Capital Bank's new headquarters in a high-rise in Miami's financial district. The Gensler team represented a close collaboration of designers from several offices in order to create the desired image.

Allied Bank, Houston, TX
Using a flexible office plan and conveying an image of tradition and openness in a dignified corporate statement, Gensler met the needs of the fast-growing Allied Bank. Open doorways and glass walls framed in mahogany and trimmed with brass beading meet the client's image requirements.

In the employee cafeteria, the existing fifty-foot high skylit space was treated with a swagged canopy above palm trees to create a "lofty lushness." Employees find this space to be an oasis during the ordinary workday.

As a more egalitarian and team-oriented spirit pervades the world of business, the firms with whom I work are concerned about providing pleasant, attractive, motivating workplaces for all their employees. Because design is a reflection of culture and attitude, clients are taking a more active interest in how best to spend their dollars, and even partners are paying more attention to the details. Typically, much of a design budget is spent in the most visible areas, but there is also an emphasis on maintaining a consistent image throughout an office and standardization becomes a tremendous benefit.

It is fascinating to me that often the most difficult constraints in a workplace project - scale, budget, schedule - are the things that push us further and make us develop something quite extraordinary. Vision is an integral part of the design process. I recognize that one of our most important missions is to help our clients see what it is they really want and need in their new work environment. In the end, the client has the facility and the design team has a sense of accomplishment, and hopefully, a long-term collaborative relationship will develop. Designing a successful work environment is an experience we share with the client, where everyone learns and everyone grows.

Designing in an Era of Continual Change

by Edward C. Friedrichs,
FAIA, IIDA

Comparing a portrait of Gensler today to my first day on the job 28 years ago is a great way to think about a period of astounding change in the architecture and design professions. I wandered into the Hearst Building on the corner of Third and Market Streets in San Francisco to join a merry band of 22 assorted architects and interior designers doing something I'd never heard of: tenant planning services. Of course, we were doing a few other types of projects as well: a large apartment complex in Newport Beach, a computer center for MasterCard in San Francisco, a restaurant at the end of the airport runway in San Diego. Gensler was the typical small architectural practice of the time, except for this extraordinary interest in something which had previously been done by real estate brokers on the back of envelopes and by furniture dealers and decorators. We had set out to accomplish a number of goals: to define and professionalize a service which hadn't existed before; to focus on design in service to our clients' business missions; to extend the layout of furniture into design in three dimensions; to be architects of the interiors (not just furniture space planners), addressing structural, mechanical, electrical, lighting, and acoustic issues with the same skill and care expected of the architect of the building shell. We've added to that the dimension of time, designing for the lifecycle of a place, searching for the answers to adaptability as businesses change.

Today, we're over 1,300 professionals in 16 offices around the world, providing a broad variety of services that continually evolve in response to our clients' need to create and manage physical (and today, virtual) space in order to enhance their business performance.

That's "what we do." How we do it may be more interesting. Lately, we've started

Wilshire Associates Santa Monica, CA
The building is a unique environmental response to a direct oceanfront orientation. The building faces due south, with an overhang at each floor that allows the windows to be undraped throughout the year so users can take full advantage of the dramatic ocean views.

playing around with a technique used for many years by Royal Dutch Shell to brainstorm organizational responses to the world they serve. Known as "Scenario Planning," the technique is best summarized in a book, *The Art of the Long View*, by Peter Schwartz. It's a process of developing multiple scenarios about all the things going on in the world around us — environmental, political, social, demographic, religious and economic — and then designing business, or in our case, service strategies, in response to each scenario. This is new stuff for us; we're not quite the size of Shell. But we seem to be culturally well suited to this approach. For the most part, our profession starts out trying to teach us to think this way, to be problem-identifiers. Other than those who become sidetracked by the Howard Roark egocentric approach to design, I think we, as architects and designers, are a pretty empathic lot.

So, if we're doing scenario planning today to help shape the types of services that will be most appropriate for the folks who purchase design services, what sort of models should we be using? Most of us have spent a generation believing that the population around the world was exploding at an unsustainable rate; that we would very rapidly, perhaps within our lifetimes, reach a level that exceeded the earth's capacity to provide food, water, and natural resources; that air quality and lifestyle would continue in a deteriorating spiral. We've lived with a constant fear of recurrent inflation or a repeat of the Great Depression. These are also the factors most of our client organizations have been using as the building blocks for their scenario planning.

Some alternative models are worth considering. Consider Roger Bootle's new book, *The Death of Inflation: Surviving and Thriving in the Zero Era*. A renowned economist who has served on the British Treasury's Panel of Independent Economic Advisors, Roger makes a compelling case that both 1929 and the inflation anomalies of the 1970s and 1980s are not likely to recur. He suggests that we think more seriously about our responses to a world economy that will cycle through a narrow band of inflation and deflation averaging zero. He points to the consequences of deflation as experienced recently in the Scandinavian countries and Japan. It's a different scenario than our economists are using as they micromanage interest rates, or than the markets hold, as evidenced by the daily skittish response to minute bits of news that might indicate a trend toward increased or decreased inflation.

Think about Ben Wattenberg's recent book, *Values Matter Most*. Ben is a demographer who provides compelling evidence that the global fertility rates are rapidly trending downward. His prediction is that the global population will top out at 8.5 billion (it was 5.8 billion in 1996). His position is that we're actually at greater risk from population decrease. Consider for example that replacement level in our population is 2.1 children per woman. Between 1990 and 1996, the U. S. fertility rate dropped from 2.08 children per woman to 1.9, and the trend appears to be continuing downward. Great Britain is at 1.78, Japan is at 1.48, China is now at 1.8, and the average of the less developed countries is 3.3 and falling. Even countries that have traditionally had high fertility rates are rapidly trending downward.

This is at substantial odds with the paradigm we've all been living with and offers some new challenges. With life expectancy extending and fewer new members of the workforce, the number of workers per beneficiary (those dependent on the current work force for support) has gone from 8.6 in 1955 to 3.3 in 1995 and is projected to be 2.0 by 2035. In other words, our social institutions will go through some dramatic changes in

Wilshire Associates, Santa Monica, CA
The board room reflects Asian influences and the firm's Pacific Rim proximity through ambient lighting, shoji screens and the prevalent use of teak (a durable wood used on many ships).

the next several decades, and those changes will alter the demand for the places we create.

Throughout my career, I've been interested in everything from the long-range planning of cities to furniture design, and just about everything in between. I consider anything which affects the way we use buildings - the places between them, and the spaces in them - as part of the design. As a result, I have been involved in the development of a practice which blends all the disciplines involved in making places, fostering an environment of interpersonal respect for each professional involved in the process, from graphics and furnishings, to engineering and technology. As designers, the quality of our work is as related to our breadth of knowledge as it is to our empathy for, and engagement of, each expert's contribution to the complex process of making the places where we work.

Interior designers must be psychologists as well as technologists, understanding people's needs and desires, as well as the sociological processes of human interaction. Along with efficiency in office design, particularly with the increased importance of technology, we must continually build our expertise in understanding the effects of the spaces we design on personal interaction and creativity. We must put ourselves in our clients' shoes as we design, trying to live as they do, worry about the things which frighten them, and anticipate the physiological responses that are fostered by the places we create.

Since I began designing offices in 1969, work methods have gone through a rapid evolution that rivals the shift from an agrarian to an industrial society that took place in the nineteenth century. The changing ways and places in which work is done have had a profound effect on our living patterns, as well as the office space we design. The changes are most often attributed to technology. But technology is only the enabler. It facilitated the rapid reduction of labor content in manufacturing and agriculture, dramatically increasing productivity. Compared to one hundred years ago, it now takes a fraction of our work effort as a society to create the food, clothing, shelter, and products we consume as a society. The length of the current strong economic cycle, with its high employment and low inflation, is fundamentally attributable to increases in technology-driven productivity; and this includes the service sector which comprises such a large proportion of our business.

As productivity in the United States accelerated after World War II, a whole new array of business services developed. Some were part of the growing manufacturing industry; others, such as banking and insurance, law and government, entertainment and leisure activities, generated a whole new set of job descriptions loosely described as "knowledge work." These new jobs have proliferated since the 1960s, creating a demand for office space. It's the continual change in the design requirements for this "knowledge work" that has fascinated me as we've developed innovative and forward-looking workplace solutions for our clients.

So much of what we did in the 1960s and 1970s preceded the influence of technology on work process design. Our clients were focused on achieving efficiency based on an industrial model of work flow. Lessons learned from industrial engineers on the factory floor were applied to office work design, a model that led to the linear flow of paper-based information and narrow, repetitive job descriptions. The goal was to design a work floor that was flexible, allowing people and desks to be moved around like

Wilshire Associates, Santa Monica, CA
The firm's CEO wanted a comfortable office with a residential feel that would take advantage of panoramic ocean views. Color tonalities, from steely grays to soft pastels, were selected to reflect the varied hues from dawn to dusk at this setting facing the Pacific Ocean.

Wilshire Associates, Santa Monica, CA
Creating a strong design statement that reflected the innovative image of this young, aggressive investment firm was critical, particularly for their recruiting efforts. Executive and Senior Associate offices were formed using angular walls and custom furnishings that were an extension of the building's architecture (also Gensler-designed).

machines in a factory as new service "product lines" were introduced. Our earliest efforts in anticipating the impact of technology in our designs of office space were for the insurance and banking businesses, where we introduced concepts of universal planning to accommodate change through technology, and accommodate the movement of people with minimal reconfiguration of space.

It wasn't until the 1990s that we saw a dramatic acceleration in the automation of repetitive work and a true break from the industrial work process analog. The manufacturing sector was actually automating repetitive tasks well before the service sector, with the rapid introduction of robotics and experiments with team manufacturing, such as with Volvo in Sweden in the 1980s.

Today, we're designing in an era of continual change driven by advances in technology. As much as anything, the proliferation of mergers and acquisitions has been to achieve an economy of scale necessary to make the enormous investments in technology required for sophisticated work process automation. New equipment in both the manufacturing and service sectors is flexible, allowing for rapid redeployment of capital investments as product mixes change. In fact, the progress toward the ability to deliver mass-produced custom products, individually tailored to personal needs but with the cost advantages of mass production, has become the Holy Grail of both product and service enterprises. Several computer companies manufacture every computer to each customer's specification; many banks tailor each mortgage to a wide range of variables to suit each borrower's unique circumstances.

The work that people do is no longer bound to a single location by virtue of a linear, physical process. People today function as team members: they're mobile; they're away from the office visiting their customers; they're in meetings; they're in classrooms. The world of nine to five is rapidly disappearing. Like the large remote factory, the corporate headquarters and regional offices located in wooded suburbs no longer connect people to the work they do. Just as factories now demand "just-in-time" delivery of material and components requiring proximity to suppliers and access to an inventory of space in the area to add, subtract or change, so offices benefit from proximity to a business district offering space flexibility, services, and infrastructure.

In fact, our design work must be adaptable, it must respond to clients whose mission and business structure are rarely foreseeable beyond eighteen months. Nearly every organization we work with today is time-driven: "How fast can I have it? Can I expand it quickly if my business grows? Can I get rid of it if my business changes? Can I alter it to satisfy a new work process?" Add to this an increasing shortage of talented and qualified knowledge workers, and some new variables enter the equation for determining both location selection and design. Locations convenient to good housing and services, along with a secure environment and neighborhood, are strong factors in recruitment and retention.

Since the recession of the late 1980s and early 1990s when "design" meant spending money for things to be "added on," communicating waste to customers and shareholders, we're seeing a resurgence in the perceived value and benefits of excellent design; not just good, efficient planning, but environments that are a source of pride and inspiration to the people who work in them.

These are places where the use of high quality materials is integral to design for adaptability and an appropriate life-cycle, not as a symbol of prestige or importance. The

Gensler, Santa Monica office
Achieving horizontal connectivity on an unusually large floorplate was paramount to the design of Gensler's Santa Monica office. The reception and conference areas are testimony to achieving a rich and distinct appearance using modest materials.

Gensler, Santa Monica office
A fluorescent light band around the floor's core provides orientation within deep spaces. Highly flexible team workstations throughout the office are enhanced by easy-access, collaborative stand-up counters.

design image of the workplace communicates a distinct meaning to customers and clients, to employees, and to the public at large. Good design and bad design have little to do with how much money is spent, but how well it is spent. The look and feel, the amenities, and the technological infrastructure all impact the performance of an organization.

While all these factors bode well for the design profession, they demand talents and focus that are quite a stretch from what most of us learned in school. We're certainly not designing only for the accolades of our peers, despite the fact that all of us still get an enormous charge when a designer whose work we admire thinks our project is great. Today we're playing for the applause of the people who work in the organizations that hire us. If they're pleased, they work more effectively; if their performance improves, the people who hired us look good and they tell their friends or hire us to do some more. That is the design firm food chain today and the skill sets are psychology, sociology, and anthropology, along with a healthy dose of corporate politics.

But the time dimension is the most important; it is where the opportunities lie for servicing our clients more broadly and effectively. In listening to our clients, we've learned that Strategic Facilities Planning is a marvelously valuable service in helping clients make decisions regarding the "where, what and when" of the physical places that house their businesses. We're trying to change the paradigm of expectations in our firm from doing things right to doing the right things. Why? Because our clients' business models are in a constant state of evolution. Nothing exactly fits a template we've used successfully before. But Strategic Facilities Planning only has value if our designers "think strategically" as they design. In other words, if they continue to focus on the "why" of the program, not just the "what."

And then there's the concern for managing the facility after it is occupied. Today's dynamics present tremendous business opportunities in creating and managing the databases, which can be a natural byproduct of the work we do for tracking systems, equipment and area allocation. We call this Gensler Information Solutions. But the greatest potential value to the client comes from the designer who is attuned to the rigors of work process change and finds greater satisfaction from both how gracefully the space responds to these demands and how great the photos look in the magazine. So, the future belongs to the designer who makes choices based on the lifecycle of the facility and based on the learning that occurs over time by using these databases in managing facilities.

Finally, the time driver offers the most potential for the profession through recapturing some of our traditional turf from the Project Management Consultants who have appeared around the country telling horror stories about irresponsible designers (since many Project Managers came from the design profession, this whole scenario is a bit suspect). As designers, we are on a two-fold mission: first to reestablish ourselves as responsible professionals who honor budgets and schedules. This is an imperative for the entire profession or we will continue to be cast into a commoditized role in our client relationships. The second is where the real business opportunity lies: taking responsible leadership in guiding the work of the complex array of enterprises — from engineering and technology consultants to vendors and contractors to government agencies — which are responsible for taking an idea to reality. The business and design opportunity belongs to the designer who accepts project performance accountability through project

Micronomics, Los Angeles, CA
Gensler capitalized on existing characteristics of a unique, 25th-floor space for its client, a legal research firm. In response to a high, sloped-glass ceiling, Gensler created towering walls that capture the volume of the space, providing support for movable shelving and ambient lighting, and flanking alcoves (examples of Gensler Furnitecture, the strategic integration of furniture and architecture) wherein research and informal meetings are conducted.

Micronomics, Los Angeles, CA
Attention to detail provides a sense of richness that can be achieved even on a modest budget. This concept is exemplified in a built-in floral vase, the content of which is dramatized by its juxtaposition before a rectangular cut-out that reveals a naturally lit research alcove.

leadership. However, leadership is not worth much unless it is infused with the same sense of purpose for the client's business mission and a deep, abiding knowledge about good design and the role it plays in enhancing that business performance. That is why the independent project manager will never deliver as much value to the client as the project leader, who is fully connected to the entire design process from Strategic Planning to Facility Management.

My call is for more education and more breadth of understanding about how the pieces that make up the lifecycle of the places we create fit together. I'm a designer but I'm convinced that good design is not even possible today until we're working in this broader definition of our profession.

I would like to end with a project, that over time has become one of my personal favorites. In the early 1980s we designed a speculative, multi-tenant office building in Santa Monica, California. We also had the opportunity to design some of the interior spaces for an investment advisory firm, Wilshire Associates. The spaces are well-integrated with the architecture, communicating a sense of building ownership to clients of Wilshire Associates, even though they're just tenants. The client once referred to us as "the BMW of interior design," which at the time seemed like the highest compliment we could be paid. The space has served our client well for nearly 15 years, continuing to adapt to the client's changing needs, communicating a clear and strong message about their culture and style, and supporting employee recruitment and retention.

Developing the Architecture of the Workplace: Gensler

by Anthony Iannacci

With this abbreviated collection of Gensler's projects for the workplace, I hope readers come away with an idea of the complexity and depth of Gensler's work in this field. The story of Gensler is clearly a story of success and unprecedented growth. As the largest interior design firm in the world, Gensler architects, designers, and planners have worked closely with many of the most prestigious and important businesses operating toady. Since its start as a three-person firm in 1965, Gensler has executed 214 million square feet of interior design and renovation, 200 million square feet of programming, 136 million square feet of architectural design and renovation, and 55 million square feet of tenant development. The firm has worked on projects covering every corner of the business world in locations throughout the United States and abroad. They have designed and planned corporate headquarters, financial and banking institutions, law firms, facilities for computer/technology industries, government offices, transportation facilities, airports, entertainment production facilities, as well as insurance companies, and facilities for petroleum and natural resources industries. In addition to these staggering statistics that are in themselves a testimony to Gensler's enormous success, there exists an underlying force to the work and an incredibly coherent common denominator. I am not here referring to a stylistic or aesthetic coherence, but instead a commitment to architecture as a political event and design as the resolution of problems.

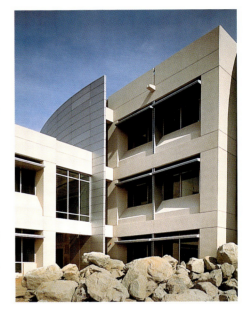

Fundamental to Gensler's process is an ability to understand which "political" issues, and here "political" refers to that which pertains to the administration of any group of people or community, a client might need to address in order to meet its business goals. Arthur Gensler started Gensler with a tenant development project in which he focused on understanding the needs of prospective tenants and then executing his design in direct response to his findings. Through this process he learned a great deal about how to communicate ideas about spaces, and that design and space planning were the primary tools that businesses had to resolve one of their most important problems: the management of their people.

Arthur Gensler's belief that an understanding of his client's business is fundamental to the design process has clearly become the key to the firm's subsequent growth and success. Gensler has developed a specialization in the architecture, design, and planning of business environments, and their goal is the advancement of their clients' business performance through architecture.

The Gensler architects and designers are acutely aware of the fact that their clients are constantly changing and that business is defined by properly guided and directed growth and flux. It becomes clear that the people at Gensler believe they as designers need to work with their clients to understand their needs; their approach, however, is not simply to ask what they need, but to discover it and uncover it. They understand that each of their projects has been motivated by change, and they try to communicate to clients their belief that the workplace is one of the key tools an organization has to support change. Whether this change is about expanding, contracting, or reallocating resources, the success of Gensler's solutions relies heavily on the understanding of their clients needs.

Epson America, Inc., Torrance, CA
For the Japanese computer company, Gensler designed both the base building and interior architecture, blending the latest technology with traditional Asian deign influence.

Jeppesen, Englewood, Colorado
One of the world's leaders in the field of aircraft navigation information Jeppesen asked Gensler to work with them in renovating and expanding their world headquarters. The goals of the project were to accommodate future expansion while maintaining flexibility for internal growth and technological advancements.

Jeppesen, Englewood, Colorado
The collective goal of both Jeppesen and Gensler was to produce a facility that provides a strong design image that represents the quality, dependability, and trustworthiness of Jeppesen to both internal and external customers.

Union Bank of Switzerland, New York, NY
Creating a ground-floor work environment, Gensler gave the client a functional space and an appropriate cultural image that is readily available to passers-by on the street.

Much of the work we are presenting within this volume is quite distant from the static, monumental architectural expression often associated with "successful" architects. This, instead, is a body of work that has responded to the constant changes in the workplace. By nature, it is the product of a rigorous collaboration that has become like all important architecture, a reflection of a larger cultural position. This body of work reflects the flexibility and dynamism of the contemporary business world while addressing its ever-changing needs. Every project arises from a compelling business decision, and the strategy implemented depends on whether their clients are facing an expiring lease, have recently merged with another company, or need to attract the best talent in the industry. But to think that change in the business world is governed only by "business" issues would be to understand only part of the process that the Gensler designers have been involved in.

The collection of projects presented here illustrates that "successful" businesses no longer function alike or look alike, and that the workplace has grown in the last thirty years into a highly specialized environment, finely tuned to meet the needs of its occupants. Gensler's architectural and design process that we are celebrating with this volume rises from the need to address complex combinations of changes in both society and business. On some level, all the work presented here addresses the new management techniques that have guided a transformation of the workplace into a more agreeable world with a newly found focus on the individual.

The Gensler architects, planners, and designers have been challenged not only by the necessity to create design solutions that could accommodate the rise in company cultural engineering, but stimulate and support it. As the international business world slowly shifted from Frederick Taylor's principles of scientific management to the Total Quality principles originally set out by W. Edwards Deming, the architecture and design of the workplace also underwent a dramatic revolution. Under the influence of a Taylorist world view, the manager's role was to overpower the worker's mind and body, not to appeal to the worker as a thinking, valuable individual. The Taylorized worker was unappreciated, easily replaceable, not encouraged to develop skills, and inexpensive to maintain. As a consequence, boredom and feelings of belittlement were common emotions at the office. Gensler's designs for the evolving workplace have been intensely informed by these issues and concerns. While the business world developed modern participative management techniques, Gensler provided the physical solutions within which newly "empowered" workers could make their own work decisions. While business attempted to recognize their employee's job accomplishments, strengthen the family-like ties between co-workers, and increase employee loyalty to the company, Gensler was faced with the challenge of creating spaces to address and foster these issues.

As large corporations and companies have attempted to occupy the role of "helpful relative" with regard to employee problems at both work and at home, Total Quality called not only for a "re-skilled" worker, but also for an "enriched" workplace. As a consequence today's workplace is quickly becoming the center of many people's lives. As the sense of community in our cities and suburban areas seems to be

diminishing constantly, the "community" of the workplace has grown ever more important. The Gensler designers understand that it is more likely that we participate in the lives of our co-workers than in the lives of our neighbors across the hall or across the street; they also understand that many of their clients must address this absence of external community by establishing a strong internal corporate culture. In the presentation of these projects, you will often encounter references to concepts such as "establishing a sense of community," "fostering the corporate culture," or "creating 'neighborhoods' within the space." When the Gensler designers use these devices, they are involved in an architectural strategy that is "political" in nature as it responds directly to the needs of the people occupying the spaces, the needs that go well beyond a pre-established "business" plan. The Gensler architects, designers, and planners understand that the workplace is in a dramatic state of change, but also understand that it is our larger culture that is the catalyst for these changes.

Gensler understands that people are working in increasingly diverse ways, and as architects of the workplace it is their job to orchestrate this diversity. The traditional office that once hosted a standardized nine-to-five work structure is rapidly giving way to other work patterns: employees are out of their workplaces a good deal of the time - on the road, in meetings, or on site with clients. Gensler, as a result, is redesigning, rethinking, and replanning the traditional work environment of single-occupancy workstations and private offices. They have planned a vast number of alternative work environments, each designed to accommodate new work patterns, and some of which we were able to document within this volume. At the same time the designers understand that people still need to work together in a community-oriented atmosphere. Therefore, their projects often call for the creation of specific areas for different activities; project rooms, quiet rooms, guest areas, as well as collaborative environments that promote teamwork and facilitate interaction among employees. At times this might mean the creation of small groupings of employees, or, at others, it might mean the creation of a large, visually open area where employees can "feel" the contact of their co-workers and observe the entire team at work.

Every business organization has a unique past, present, and future, and Gensler, therefore, tailors its solutions to the unique and individual qualities of each client. There is an awareness of the forces of change affecting the way people work, and consequently, how office environments should be planned and designed. For the Gensler designers, the biggest challenge lies in understanding the client's business and to forming a partnership in order to accurately meet the facilities' needs. Readers will notice that the Gensler team of architects, designers, and planners have worked carefully on the creation of standards which are then applied to field-specific workplaces such as law firms, for example. But while such standards can be quite useful, they can only be applied in certain areas of their work. As the business world moves at an accelerated rate, the Gensler designers are challenged by the requirements of some of the world's fastest growing companies that are expanding into completely new territories where office standards simply do not exist.

The Gensler designers focus on finding out what their

Perkins Coie, Seattle, WA
Main library. Organized by floor, each of the nine practice groups has a subject-specific library.

Morrison & Foerster, Palo Alto, CA
Despite the increasing dependence on technology for document generation and storage, law firms continue to have the internal library as an essential element.

Chevron Corporation, San Francisco, CA
Work spaces can apply to the chairman's offices as well. Considerations of efficient planning, comfort, and proper image are given consideration.

Davis Polk & Wardwell, New York, NY
The 11 practice floors are connected by a convenient stair punctuated with reception areas at every other floor. Increased communication among various practice groups has become a major consideration in law office design.

client's needs are, where the client hopes to go, what is required to get there, and then on developing the strategies to deliver the services which meet those needs. As part of their approach to workplace architecture Gensler is involved in strategic planning. As architectural consultants, they often help clients understand how to use their real estate and facilities as strategic tools for optimum human performance. By being involved in this early research process, the designers are provided with the information necessary to identify the problems and create the appropriate design solutions. The people at Gensler try to communicate to their business clients that good workplace design must consider and employ all available resources - people, time, money, information, technology and space - to their fullest potential. Their clients grow to understand that they can compete through the services, location, and design that they offer their employees, and it is for this reason that Gensler has established so many long-term relationships with its various clients.

The Gensler designers attempt to exemplify that high standards of planning and design are the result of building effective solutions that directly impact an organization by adding value and enhancing the environment and well-being of employees. Good design carries a sense of "ownership," "belonging," and "privilege;" if a space is well designed one feels important and a sense of value becomes associated with one's work, position, and production. Through Gensler's efforts, many of their clients now view workplace design as one of the many tools that an organization may depend on to reach its strategic goals.

Today's architects of the workplace are also challenged by the need to create design solutions that reflect the specific identity of their users. The Gensler designers must understand their clients physical and technological needs, but they must also understand the "character" of their client. They have learned to interpret their clients requirements, position within the market, competition, and resources, and like highly-skilled musicians they bring to each interpretation new expression. Among their greatest strengths, is their ability to create workplace environments that become part of their client's ongoing process of growth, change, and self-definition. As a result of this finely-tuned interpretation, their design solutions do not stem from ready-made kit parts that simply result in static, standard solutions. Rather, the Gensler designers aim to create exceptional workplace environments that reflect the partnerships they create with their clients and their commitment to rise above the mediocrity of standard solutions.

Gensler has clearly developed the architecture of the workplace by creating vital and appropriate solutions for their client's workplace needs. They believe that effective design solutions are the result of understanding work practices, organizational culture, and physical space. While aesthetics and cost may have been the cornerstones for workplace design in the recent past, workplace planning is currently driven by new issues. Any business, regardless of its location, is facing challenges: rapid technological developments, dramatically shorter schedules, increasingly complex environmental concerns, employee concerns, the changing work force, and global competition. As architects of the workplace, the Gensler team embraces these concerns to create design solutions that are informed by them.

Projects

The Prudential Insurance Company of America's western headquarters in Westlake, California, was designed and developed according to standards typical of all Prudential projects conceived in the late 1970s. For the development of this facility, Prudential established a team of their corporate headquarters' staff members and a local Prudential facilities group along with outside architectural and interior design firms. Throughout the design process, the Prudential team not only oversaw the development, but also stood by to insure that all corporate guidelines were met.

The three-story, 755-foot-long building with more than 400,000 square feet of gross space broke ground in 1979. The wedge-like structure was gracefully set into the natural terrain on forty-nine landscaped and master-planned acres within a sixty-four-acre parcel of land. At the heart of the interior of the structure, the architects placed a full-height, skylight-capped atrium that spans the entire length of the building. The interior design surrounding the dramatic space allows individuals to move along its perimeters and provides visual access into each of the floors. **The Prudential project represents one of the first open atriums used in an office building and can be considered a landmark in the development of the interior space used to create a sense of community.**

When commenting on his work for Prudential, Edward C. Friedrichs, then managing principal of Gensler's Los Angeles office, stated that his "main concerns in the interior design, in addition to respecting the architecture, were flexibility to meet changing office needs, human orientation in very large spaces, and timelessness." This notion of proper orientation within a vast space and the creation of interiors on a human scale became the foundation for many of the design principles the Gensler team used throughout the Prudential space.

Prudential Insurance built its new facility because the company was outgrowing existing offices, and recognized a need to more efficiently organize the flow of their work. In their other facilities, various divisions of the company, although working together, were often separated within the space, creating lapses in communication. **The challenge of designing the 400,000-square-foot office space was to simultaneously enhance the level of communication between each of the departments and achieve a higher level of flexibility for the entire space.** The Gensler team developed an interior that is completely open in concept. The main circulation system is located parallel to the central axis of the building, and creates a "street" along which service functions and meeting places are located.

Gensler incorporated a modular concept throughout the building to achieve maximum flexibility. Carpeting, interior partitions, seating, and wood casework in private offices all reflect the overall organizing plan. A new desk system, designed to accommodate the use of CRT equipment at each workstation, was developed specifically for the project by the Gensler design team and Bruce Hannah, and

Prudential Insurance Company of America

The building angles to conform to the site. An executive mandate for the building called for long floors in order to expedite workflow.

Facing page
A full-length, full-height and dramatic atrium is flooded with natural light from skylight. The atrium not only enlivens the building interior, but also affords control of long floors required for workflow efficiency.

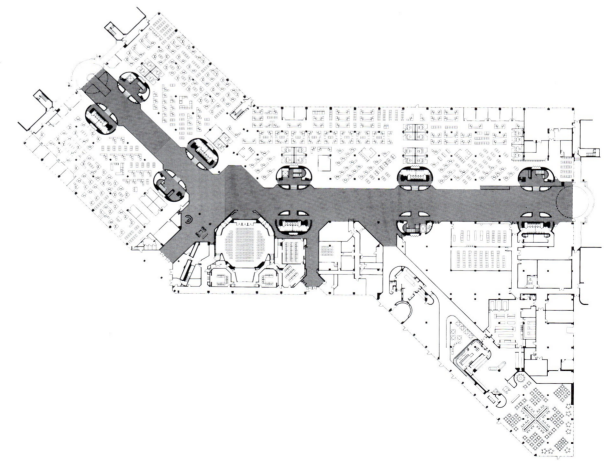

Nine bridges span the atrium, connecting major pathways. Large columns, placed at regular intervals along the sides of the atrium, anchor the glass-sided bridges.

Prudential's headquarters is constructed in five isolated sections to withstand seismic activity. The exterior, faced with panels of Carnelian granite, is gracefully set into natural terrain.

A view into the informal seating area of the major sawtoothed spline atrium reveals soft natural light coming through north light monitors.

was produced by Knoll. These low desks, later referred to as the Hannah system, include detachable wire management panels that can be altered easily to accommodate different tasks without having to be moved. The extremely functional nature of this prototype addressed the client's need to adapt work areas to meet a wide variety of requirements.

In order to develop a sense of identity for the smaller work units dispersed along the extensive, open floors flanking the atrium, the Gensler designers created specific "neighborhoods" for the numerous departments. These zones were articulated by the placement of large-scale service pods containing copy machines and supplies as well as space for processing incoming and outgoing mail. The designers also worked with the placement of full-height conference rooms throughout the space and carpet squares in varied colors to articulate different departmental areas and circulation paths. **Gensler's main concern for the design of the interior spaces was to establish a human scale with a sense of community while maintaining the very large, open spaces.** In order to keep vistas free of visual barriers, banks of tall filing cabinets were placed only near cores and columns, and private offices and conference rooms line up with service cores. Support areas are surrounded by low partitions, and file cabinets are topped only with plants to divide large areas without breaking up the space.

The zones from the circulation path to the atrium were designed for employees who tend to work independently of others, with workstations placed on the diagonal. The clear circulation paths also permitted the designers to employ an automated mail delivery system. By the use of a special transparent chemical placed on the carpet, a mail-mobile, a robotic device that delivers and picks up mail, is able to travel from one mail station to another within the departments without human assistance.

Working from the premise that successful communication could be attained by organizing people in effective working situations, the designers complied with the senior executives' decision to omit workstation divider panels. Friedrichs explains, "they wanted direct eye contact between manager and employee, as well as among employees themselves." This "open" space was designed to reflect Westlake's management style of operations and immediately created an environment of collaboration. Though this arrangement appeared contrary to the traditional use of panel screens for acoustical privacy, the activity of so many people working in the space created enough masking noise to obscure individual conversations. In addition to interior design and planning, the Gensler team also provided a building manual detailing standards, drawings for workstation and private office configurations, supplier names, finishes, and planning concepts. The manual allowed the client to continue to maintain its facility after its move-in date.

The cafeteria wing, which includes an outdoor dining deck, comfortably seats nearly 400 at a time.

Staff lounge adjacent to cafeteria offers employees a pleasant environment for informal get-togethers, an important part of Prudential's corporate culture.

Conference room has glass on two sides and affords views onto a typical workstation area.

Vice president office located on the perimeter of the building. Vice presidents participated by choosing their furniture, office layout, and art work.

Secretarial workstations are located outside glass-fronted private offices to afford visual communication.

After completing their successful Pennzoil Place project in 1976, architects Philip Johnson and John Burgee designed the RepublicBank Center for a nearby site in downtown Houston. At the time of Johnson and Burgee's involvement with the RepublicBank project, the bank saw itself in a position of economic prestige comparable to that of the guilds of Northern Europe in the fifteenth century. The Gothic guildhall became a point of departure for Johnson and Burgee who brought these older elements into a postmodern context. The bank sought to associate itself with Houston's rich downtown surroundings, while contrasting itself with an equally powerful design, representing RepublicBank's formidable presence. While initiating a contemporary dialogue with historical appropriation, the building's red granite facade, pitched roof, and highly crafted, graceful lead finials also stood in clear stylistic opposition to Houston's many Modernist glass towers. Located directly across Louisiana Street from Pennzoil Place, the RepublicBank Center is a dynamic, low-level structure hosting the main banking hall and a high-rise office tower.

Confident in Gensler's creative ability to continue the rich and venerable dialogue of the exterior architecture and site planning, the bank engaged the firm to create a design for the interiors that would reinforce the powerful building architecture without overpowering its occupants. Working with the building architects, Gensler adapted many architectural details from the secular Gothic style for the interior spaces of this modern bank. The team used granite extensively throughout the space to reinforce the motifs of the building architecture, creating a sense of continuity between the exterior and the interior spaces. Gensler also incorporated granite arches and made extensive use of wood. They designed plaster barrel vaulted ceilings that run the length of the major circulation corridors. Within these vaulted ceilings, concealed neon lights provide uniform illumination. The vast banking hall is constructed in the Dutch Gothic style with spectacular 125-foot ceilings where natural light filters down through skylights. **The Gensler designers were faced with the challenge of establishing an environment that would simultaneously celebrate this dramatic space as the core of the building's architecture and address the functional needs of the most public area of the bank.**

Antony Harbour, then managing principal of Gensler's Houston office, explained that "one goal for the banking hall design was to avoid creating a space that looked like a church." **The designers brought elements typically associated with exterior urban spaces into their design for the banking hall and the public spaces in order to establish a sense of the dynamic within the lofty spaces.** Throughout the project the interior design functions as an aesthetic and functional filter between the dichotomy of the retrospection of historical quotation and the progressive position of contemporary banking. For example, the Gensler team placed a seventy-year-old four-faced clock, chosen by Gerald

RepublicBank of Houston

The plan shows how the 12-story banking hall rises behind the 53-story tower. The tower steps up twice to create the illusion of three towers.

Looking across banking hall. The vaulted arcade that joins the banking hall to the tower's elevator lobby bisects the first five floors of the tower.

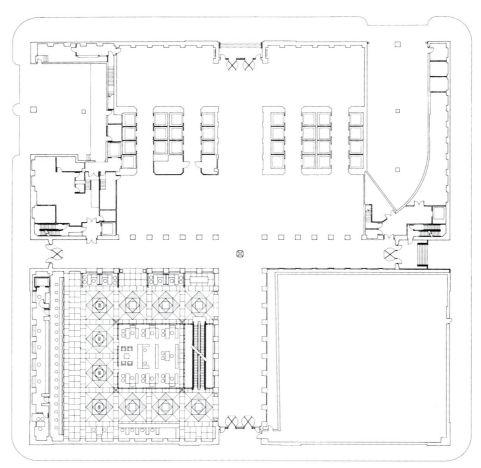

Black iron rails surround the new accounts area located in the center of the banking hall with one 17-foot-high street lamp at each of the four corners.

D. Hines Interests, at an important intersection between the banking hall and the high-rise of RepublicBank Center. Also, seventeen-foot-high traditional cast iron street lamps are used to provide supplemental light within the space of the banking hall. These "historical" symbols signal the overall historical quotations of the building's architecture, while setting the stage for the modern activities occurring within the bank.

At one end of the banking hall the designers placed a long line of teller windows. Black iron rails, with twisting and curving ball-capped elements, surround the customer service area in the center of the hall and the mezzanine above. The railings, much like the street lamps and four-faced clock, convey a sense of both human scale and urban dynamism into the space. The interiors have Josef Hoffmann-designed seating, which was chosen for its grand scale and placed within the customer service area and throughout many of the office spaces. For the floor of the bank hall, the designers created a geometric pattern of red, black, and pearl granite that both echoes the architecture of the space and indicates patterns of circulation.

The designers located training areas and the employee cafeteria on the fourth floor of the rectangular high-rise. Four rooms in this area were designed specifically as classrooms for the bank's extensive training program and were conceived with maximum flexibility in mind. One is equipped with audiovisual equipment and video monitors designed specifically for role-playing exercises. Located down the corridor from the employee cafeteria, large groups of people can meet in these training areas and adjourn for breaks without disrupting other bank employees.

The executive suite on the fifth floor hosts one of the bridges that spans from the arcade to the banking hall and visually connects this private area to the public space below. The rectangular shape of the building helps maximize the efficiency of the executive space, allowing private offices to be located around the entire perimeter of the building. For this area the Gensler team designed a boardroom, private dining rooms with small adjacent kitchens, Executive Vice President offices, and the Chairman of the Board and President's offices. The executive boardroom was designed with complete audiovisual capabilities including rear-screen projection. The lights were designed with dimmers that are automatically set at the proper light level for meetings, dining, slide shows, speeches, etc. **Always with flexibility in mind, the designers created a boardroom table that is actually made of twenty-six individual tables that can separate to be arranged in a variety of configurations.**

Throughout the offices, the Gensler designers concealed raceways behind wooden doors and panels. These raceways were established for computer and word processing cables that run vertically through the building up to the computer center on the thirteenth floor and the word processing center on the fifteenth floor. This system allows individuals on any floor to install a terminal at a desk or workstation simply by running the necessary wires to the raceway where they can be connected with a cable leading up to these two centers.

Reduction of office sizes, initially a response to the high construction costs for the project, became a positive innovation in the design and planning of the space. The Gensler designers scaled the standard office size down from ten by fifteen feet, to ten by thirteen feet and decreased the width of the corridors to five feet. In order to maintain a sense of spaciousness, the designers then recessed the doorway two feet into the office. The recession of the doorway creates a unique vestibule at each entryway and a niche within the office by enlarging the corridor in higher traffic areas and providing the necessary visual relief in the long narrow space. As the designers established this niche they rotated the traditional orientation of the office by 180 degrees. This meant that the occupant's desk no longer faced the doorway, but rather, the window. The credenza supporting the data processing equipment was placed in the niche opposite the window wall. The designers found that this arrangement screened the office occupant and eliminated the distractions of pedestrian traffic. It was also found that the doors on private offices were seldom used and remained open over ninety-five percent of the time. As a consequence for this project, those offices having no functional privacy requirement were not provided with doors. Instead there are numerous conference rooms for those occasions when individuals whose offices do not have doors need space to conduct private meetings and conversations.

Boardroom with reconfigurable custom table. Smaller conference rooms are strategically located to allow easy access for impromptu meetings or one-on-one meetings.

Seating area on the banking hall level has views to the elegant strength of the interior architecture.

A plaster barrel-vaulted ceiling runs the length of the main corridors of the executive space on level 5. The ceiling is an interpretation of the vaulted ceiling in the banking hall and continues the 17th Century style.

Plans for levels 3 and 5 show that typical office floors have large floorplates and 250-foot-long corridors. Bank management opted to remain within a primarily closed plan since "customers want privacy."

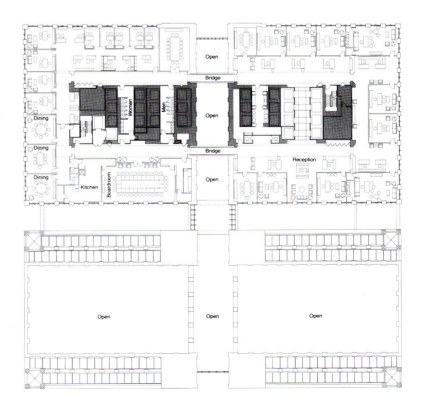

One open plan workspace houses a lending group, whose staff visits prestigious clients at their own offices, minimizing the need for privacy on the bank's premises.

Support area outside enclosed office. Bank management opted to remain with a primarily closed office plan. As a large commercial bank whose main activity is lending to other businesses, the bank has many customers who want the privacy of an enclosed space.

While many food establishments are readily accessible within the Houston underground system, the bank provided an employee cafeteria as an added amenity.

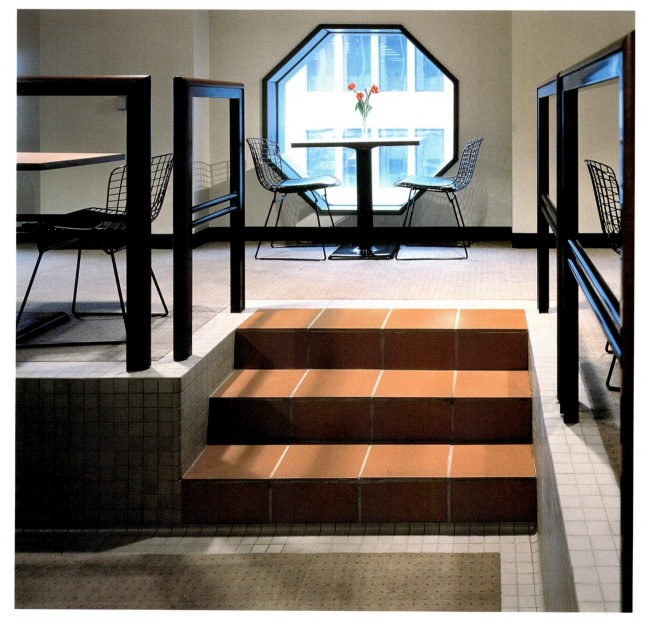

Gensler seized the opportunity created by doorless offices to introduce interesting architectural elements in the recessed doorways.

Goldman, Sachs & Company, one of the first full-service, global investment banking firms, currently employs approximately 9,000 people from 90 countries in offices located throughout the United States and in many of the world's financial centers. Founded in 1869 by Marcus Goldman, an immigrant from Europe, as a commercial paper dealership, Goldman Sachs today remains one of the few major financial organizations structured as a private partnership. **With a strong focus on client service, the firm was also the first to set up a group devoted solely to marketing the full range of the firm's services and to ensuring continuity of client relationships.** Goldman Sachs was one of the first Wall Street firms to recruit MBAs and formed Wall Street's first Mergers & Acquisitions and Real Estate departments.

Since the late 1970s, Gensler has worked with Goldman Sachs on three major projects: its 85 Broad Street facility in New York City, the European headquarters in the Peterborough Court building on Fleet Street in London, and at One New York Plaza. For each of these projects, the Gensler interior architects, planners, and designers saw a number of common characteristics:

1. The partners' full participation and support in developing the highest quality of overall design approach.
2. The use of full-scale mock-ups to evaluate all significant components of the space.
3. Space requirements for universal flexibility, with hierarchical status downplayed.
4. Accommodation of environmental considerations - building mechanical systems and controls, comfort level, security, cabling, and communications.
5. Building a number of extra conference rooms, sized for easy conversion into vice president and partner offices (if necessary).
6. Emphasis on amenities - full-service staff cafeterias, training facilities (that continue to expand) and client dining/conferencing spaces, and a rotating art program
7. Providing fast internal communications on three levels - visual, verbal, and physical (through staircases).
8. Implementation by their in-house facilities group, who manage the spaces upon completion of the projects.

As investment banking experienced dynamic growth in the 1980s and 1990s, Goldman Sachs has continued to modify, restack and replan their facilities; and ultimately took over tenancy of the entire building at 85 Broad Street. The London facility has proven to be equally successful, and it has gone to nearly full occupancy of the Peterborough Court building. The Goldman Sachs partners continue to maintain a very high level of interest in the planning and design in all Goldman Sachs facilities and have maintained a relationship with Gensler as their needs change and facilities evolve.

Goldman, Sachs & Company

On entering a typical reception area, a visitor's first impression is one of welcome. Artwork is placed in almost every public space.

Corridor view into private office. Furnishings were reused in private offices, conference rooms and wherever else possible.

85 Broad Street, New York
By 1979 Goldman Sachs had experienced such rapid growth that the partners decided not only that they needed a new, consolidated headquarters in a new thirty-story building designed by Skidmore, Owings & Merrill, but they also wanted the work environment to appropriately reflect their firm culture. The partners, numbering over 60, considered it of significant value to the firm to focus their energy on creating the appropriate facility, both from a functional and, equally important, an overall design perspective.

Goldman Sachs retained Gensler to provide full interior architectural design services, including building analysis, programming, development of corporate standards, and a complete graphic design program for the consolidation and renovation of the corporate headquarters. To accomplish this goal, Goldman Sachs formed a Space Committee made up of two components: partners who ran the various business units (mergers and acquisitions, equities, fixed income, research, investment banking, real estate, operations, comptroller, etc.) to strategize; and a facilities group to implement those decisions. As teamwork is an important part of the Goldman Sachs firm culture, the Gensler team served as an equal partner on the project, working hand-in-hand with the Goldman Sachs Space Committee.

The 85 Broad Street project was the first time that Goldman Sachs had taken such a systematic approach to the design of one of their facilities, since there had previously been no focused effort to do so; they simply expanded as they needed, taking a little more space here and there. This new strategy, based on the realization that good design and planning can enhance employee performance and satisfaction, became the standard for all future facilities projects. The Goldman Sachs partners were interested in every aspect of the design and strongly supported Gensler's programming efforts. **The partners wanted to ensure that the new space would support the firm's long-range business goals and represent its democratic culture, where people are considered the firm's most important resource.**

One of the first project initiatives was to help refine many components of the base building structure and systems. Early in the process, Gensler's collaboration with the base building architects allowed for the identification of ideal locations for the trading floors, special ceilings, and other essential elements that were factored into the building. By including special requirements for trading facilities, computers, and food service areas in the base building, the design and construction addressing these special concerns were simplified and could be implemented more economically and efficiently.

The Gensler team worked extensively on the core areas to provide consistent locations for reception areas and access points to all floors. Based on Gensler's recommendations, the building core on each floor was modified to incorporate not only

Goldman, Sachs & Company, New York

85 Broad Street, 1982
Typical Floor plan with identified "growth space" demonstrates the way Goldman Sachs dealt with room for expansion. The facility was planned so tightly, that a specific space was designated for future occupancy as needed. Within six months of move-in, all growth space was absorbed.

Facing page
85 Broad Street, 1982
Client hospitality, an important component of the Goldman Sachs culture, is accomodated in an elegant, comfortable private dining area.

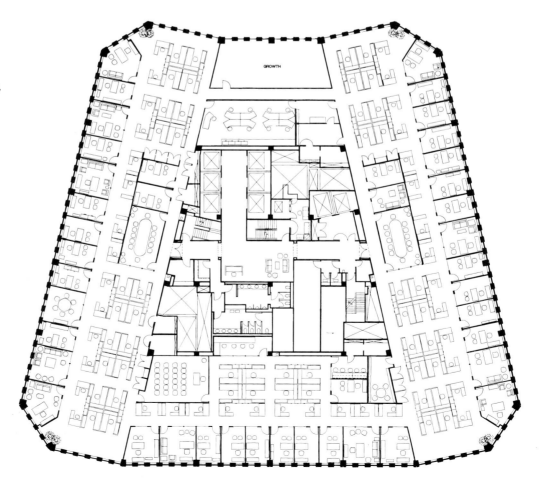

specialized security needs, communication systems, HVAC, wind bracing, etc., but also all support elements such as reception, conveyor, mailroom, coffee pantry and communicating stair. This new plan took full advantage of the forty-five-foot-wide column-free office area around the core.

A significant project challenge was to incorporate the different - and increased - technology requirements of the various trading groups, and Gensler identified opportunities within the building structure itself. Trading facilities were located on the upper floors of the building and additional HVAC systems installed to handle the increased load. In addition to lowering trading floor slabs to create increased ceiling heights and eliminate ramps, the designers reinforced the library and computer floors and significantly increased telephone, power, and data cable rise capacity. Four new sets of risers installed on each corner of the core permitted telephone and electrical wiring to be run under the floors throughout the building, an innovation that at the time was considered state-of-the-art, as it simplified these services and made them more accessible to users.

For the project, which included over one million square feet of building space, Gensler applied a consistent planning module to facilitate future needs while maintaining high standards of quality at all levels. The designers instituted a very simple hierarchy in terms of private offices, designed in only two sizes: one for partners and one for vice presidents. The Goldman Sachs partners were given monetary allowances to decorate their glass-fronted offices, which were designed for maximum utility, incorporating adequate filing space and technology requirements. The remaining staff were then located in systems of open plan workstations and color schemes were used as a way to distinguish each business unit. Having come from an environment with conventional desks and vintage chairs, Goldman Sachs employees found this innovation significantly improved the quality of the environment and aided in the creation of a corporate community.

In keeping with the democratic firm culture, the Goldman Sachs partners required that the overall interior design of the headquarters should emphasize employee amenities. Gensler was encouraged to establish the same level of quality throughout the work environment, with no delineation between back-of-office and front-of-office space. The headquarters includes a full-service employee cafeteria, training facilities, and auditorium featuring specialized audiovisual and teleconferencing systems. Client services are located on a portion of one of the upper floors, with space dedicated to client dining rooms as well as much-needed conference rooms. An extensive permanent and rotating art collection was an essential element of the overall design.

The Goldman Sachs partners also believed that staff should have a say in, for example, the kind of chair they would be sitting in all day. Working with a pilot group from Goldman Sachs, Gensler created a

85 Broad Street, 1982
The majority of the staff is located in open plan systems furniture workstations that were selected to enhance flexibility, reflect the firm's culture, and provide functional and flexible work areas.

series of full-scale mock-ups to test numerous details of the office environment - office sizes, office fronts, furniture, lighting, finishes, etc. - on the basis of performance, aesthetics, comfort, functionality, ergonomics and cost. The team paid special attention to the trading desk mock-up, which would be used for 410 trading positions. They evaluated lighting, environmental controls due to increases in equipment temperature, sizes of computer screens, and, even then, the concept of emerging flat screen technology (which is yet to be put to widespread use).

Gensler's involvement at 85 Broad Street did not end with the move-in. The designers continued their relationship with Goldman Sachs to ensure that this client enjoyed an appropriate, and functional, work environment at 85 Broad Street. As Goldman Sachs grew and expanded operations, Gensler worked on strategic space planning and facilities design for the financial firm at other locations, including One New York Plaza.

One New York Plaza, New York

Goldman Sachs New York continued to expand both operations and staff, and in the early 1990s Gensler was given the assignment to relocate the firm's equities group from 85 Broad Street to One New York Plaza. Gensler was asked to plan and design approximately 240,000 square feet of space on eight floors that would house trading facilities, office support, and conference/dining facilities with seating for 270 people, six additional private dining rooms, a health care facility, and a theater/teleconferencing facility expandable to accommodate 167 people. Goldman Sachs wanted Gensler to model the design of this new space along the aesthetics of the London office rather than the more traditional (i.e. elevator lobbies with wainscoting and traditional reception desks) at 85 Broad Street.

Much as they had for their previous Goldman Sachs projects, the Gensler designers adhered to the two standards for open workstations and the two standards for the glass-fronted private offices and created full-scale mock-ups for to evaluate various components. While incorporating the soft aesthetics of a subdued color palette, the designers were able to accommodate Goldman Sachs' requirement for intensive technology and information-sharing capabilities.

The designers located trading facilities on the top three floors of the building. A large equities trading facility created on the building's top floor (where ceiling heights reach nearly twelve feet) features a custom-designed coffered acoustic ceiling and lighting system, and Gensler removed all structural columns in order to achieve large open spaces. Within this trading area, the latest stock information, while available on desktop, is also shown on prominent data display boards, enhancing the level of excitement, open communication and energy.

85 Broad Street, 1982 Partners' conference room. With a strong focus on client service, Goldman Sachs today remains one of the few major financial organizations structured as a private partnership.

One New York Plaza, 1995
Density and proximity were stressed in the planning of this Equities Division Trading Floor, the heart of Goldman Sachs' Equities Division. Gensler created a mock-up to evaluate the proposed trading desk sizes, lighting, environmental controls, window coverings, and location of data screens. The resulting plan tripled the contiguous space from the 85 Broad Street trading facility.

One New York Plaza, 1995
Whether for a Vice President or Managing Director, all private offices have glass fronts and adhere to standards developed for the original 85 Broad Street headquarters.

One New York Plaza, 1995
Inclusion of a private client dining room in the tightly planned space demonstrates Goldman Sachs' focus on customer service and employee amenities. A full-service staff cafeteria and a multi-purpose auditorium are also located on this floor.

One New York Plaza, 1995
Plan of typical floor, with private offices and small conference rooms strategically located.

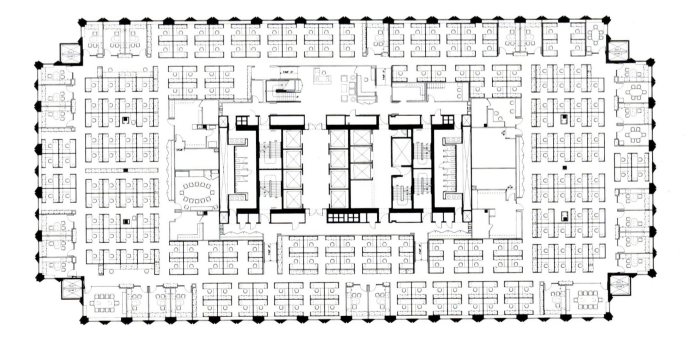

Goldman Sachs International Ltd., London

Goldman Sachs continued their dynamic growth throughout the 1980s. In 1988 Goldman Sachs International decided to improve operations and cost efficiency by consolidating all business groups, which had been located in three buildings, each with different space standards and varying levels of quality, into one facility. They retained Gensler to assist in the interior planning and design of a new ten-story headquarters facility in London's financial district. Goldman Sachs had several goals in mind for this new Kohn Pedersen Fox-designed Peterborough Court. **They wanted the new workplace to both help blend the American culture of the firm with the European environment of London's financial district and to further enhance Goldman Sachs' image as a major international financial institution.** In keeping with Goldman Sachs' emphasis on the employee, the headquarters facility also includes a training center, staff cafeteria, and small fitness facility.

The Gensler team collaborated with Kohn Pedersen Fox to improve the building's core design and systems for better efficiency. Working with the building architects, Gensler created interior spaces that would meet Goldman Sachs' technology and food service needs and also developed an office infrastructure to meet the financial firm's constantly changing space and technology requirements. Having been involved from an early stage in the project, Gensler was able to realize significant savings in terms of time and costs by incorporating construction of the interior into some contracts for the base building. In addition, Gensler not only integrated many of the exterior materials, such as wood and stone, into the interior architectural design, giving cohesion to the overall design and establishing a strong image for Goldman Sachs, but also created a strong interior connection with the detailed architecture and grid-like fenestration of the base building.

For Goldman Sachs' Peterborough Court headquarters, Gensler established a contemporary, elegant design vocabulary, which stands in direct contrast to the more traditional look they designed for the firm's Wall Street offices. **Goldman Sachs expressed the importance of having sufficient conference areas and client meeting rooms, as the nature of their European business requires more space for client hospitality and many meetings and presentations occur during mealtimes.** In response to this need, the Gensler designers placed most of the meeting and dining facilities on the building's top floor. In creating this dedicated conferencing floor, the primary design challenge for the Gensler team arose from the irregular shape of the building and the thirty-five-foot-high vaulted space, a dimension that is hardly appropriate for the scale of space required for client meetings. Gensler was able to scale down the space, while retaining the dramatic views of the City of London, by installing lower or secondary ceilings of various heights. The Gensler designers dropped the ceiling down to eight feet for the floor's elevator

Goldman Sachs International Ltd.

Peterborough Court, 1990
View into seating area of main reception area. The custom carpet is patterned after the building footprint. Gensler designed the pendant lighting fixtures.

Peterborough Court, 1990
View into main reception area shows how powerfully the gridded fenestration of the building architecture influences the interior spaces.

lobby, which leads directly into a domed rotunda, which then opens into the dramatic thirty-five-foot-high reception area. This reception area is flanked by a pair of client dining rooms, which are directly accessible if a larger meeting area is required. Twelve dining and meeting rooms, each with secondary ceiling heights proportionate to the size of the individual rooms, were created off corridors that lead from the reception area. Within these corridors, open white lacquer grills create a ceiling plane that provides a glimpse of the vault above, while humanizing the scale of the space. Each turn in the corridor is punctuated by an additional domed rotunda.

As with the other Goldman Sachs facilities, technology accommodation was a critical element in planning the London headquarters, and by the late 1980s, office products had reached a level that addressed the highly evolved technology required by Goldman Sachs. In addition, the London project adapted many of the same office standards that were developed for the 85 Broad Street facility, including only two sizes of private offices (for partners and vice presidents), although here a neutral and universal color palette was used for future flexibility. These private offices were specifically planned to house furniture that permitted a team to gather around the P-shaped desk with workwall for informal meetings and collaboration. The glass front of the office allowed people to be seen and to see activity outside the office.

Throughout the project, Gensler did extensive research on international products to be specified, especially furniture standards that supported Goldman Sachs' need for flexibility and superior aesthetics. While initially there was some resistance to creating a full-scale office mock-up, the Goldman Sachs partners supported the effort, especially since it allowed them to test a number of alternative products. Based on reactions to the mockups, REFF, a Canadian manufacturer (now part of Knoll), was determined to be the best resource. For both the US and London facilities, workstation configurations were limited to two, and specific groups were given either high or low partitions, depending on their need for visual and verbal communication and storage requirements.

Gensler's design for the Goldman Sachs International Ltd. Facility at Peterborough Court was recognized as one of the "Best in Bank and Office Design" in the *Interiors* magazine 1992 design awards competition.

Peterborough Court, 1990
Interconnecting stair is located within the security envelope created by Gensler to allow all floors to have unmanned reception areas.

Peterborough Court, 1990
Floor plan showing a trading floor and trading support/workstations.

Peterborough Court, 1990
A view of St. Paul's Cathedral from the Partners' Meeting Room.

Peterborough Court, 1990
The London project used many of the same office standards that were developed for the 85 Broad Street facility, with only two sizes of private offices (for partners and vice presidents).

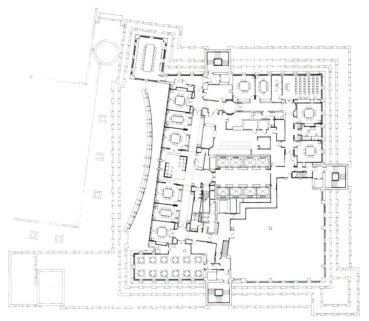

Peterborough Court, 1990
The plan for the tenth floor shows reception area, left of center, flanked by dining rooms.

Peterborough Court, 1990
The partners supported creating a full-scale private office mock-up, especially since it allowed them to test a number of alternative and equally attractive products.

Peterborough Court, 1990
Workstation configurations were limited to two, and groups were given either high or low partitions, depending on their need for visual and verbal communication and storage needs.

Peterborough Court, 1990
The unusually high slab-to-slab space in the London build-to-suit allowed Gensler to incorporate coffered ceilings and indirect lighting in the trading floor. As a result of this successful strategy in London, the trading floor in One New York Plaza also was designed with coffered ceilings.

Peterborough Court, 1990
One of the numerous private dining rooms.
Client hospitality is an important function in the London facility, where many client meetings take place over meals.

Peterborough Court, 1990
This training/meeting space located on Level B2 of the London facility was actually "found space" and was not initially planned for occupancy. The space can be reconfigured to accommodate a variety of functions.

Peterborough Court, 1990
Largest client conference/dining room. The London Goldman Sachs partners had a strong voice in planning and designing the facility, recognizing the effect of design on the company's operation.

Peterborough Court, 1990
Initial plans did not include a staff canteen, but recognizing Goldman Sachs' concern for employees, Gensler carved out space on level B1 to accommodate both the cafeteria and a small fitness center.

Enron Corp

Enron Corp operates the largest integrated natural gas pipeline system in the United States, selling and transporting about fifteen percent of all gas delivered to the nation's users via over 38,000 miles of pipeline. The company was founded in 1985 through the merger of Houston Natural Gas, Florida Gas, and InterNorth.

Houston Natural Gas first approached Gensler to discuss the design for a 350,000-square-foot headquarters building in downtown Houston. Gensler's involvement with the project began with a meeting with Enron's senior vice president to determine the company's primary requirements, formulate basic floor plans, identify optimal building shapes, and locate and evaluate buildings that would meet those needs. Predetermined criteria included financial considerations, available square footage, contiguous floors, and quality of base building finishes. In the midst of the planning phase, the various companies merged, forming Enron Corp. After several weeks of research, Four Allen Center was selected as the site for the new Enron headquarters.

Enron's new headquarters provided an opportunity for the company to establish a new corporate identity. After the merger, Enron's space requirements increased significantly and eventually rose to over one million square feet. Enron Corp would expand into all of the existing building's fifty floors to accommodate its 3,200 employees. Gensler was commissioned to design the Enron Corp headquarters on a two-year schedule from inception to move-in, a challenging timetable for any large project, but the situation was compounded by continuous changes at Enron.

At the time, Enron Corp was clearly at the center of Houston's broadening economic base and was innovative in its desire to focus on the human context of its business activities instead of outdoing everyone else with the opulence of its executive floors. Enron's chairman and CEO instructed the Gensler architects and designers to create an atmosphere that would be "warm and bright, light and friendly" in order to convey the message that Enron valued its people. **Gensler's work for Enron Corp was so innovative for the time that the project eventually created new standards for employee work environments. Throughout the project, concern for human needs in the workplace and state-of-the-art technical mastery of Enron's business activities became key factors in Gensler's establishment of a design vocabulary.** In order to meet the deadline and work effectively with Enron management, a special Gensler team was assigned to each aspect of the headquarters project—executive floor, cafeteria, computer area, health facility, typical floors, graphic design, and employee facilities.

After studying the base building selected for the new headquarters, which was originally designed for multi-tenant use, the Gensler team made numerous changes in order to accommodate the specific needs of Enron and to make optimal use of the available space on each floor. The executive floors, for example, featured twenty-two-foot high ceilings – dramatic, but overscaled for an office space.

Series of rectilinear forms for the entrance to the executive offices on the 50th floor. The mezzanine bridge with brass railing is in polyester high gloss lacquer.

Looking down into executive secretaries area from mezzanine bridge.

The volume was reduced by the addition of a mezzanine which took advantage of the full ceiling height. Secretarial space was added and a two-story executive reception area was created. The designers were able to maintain the drama of the executive spaces while simultaneously creating some 10,000 additional square feet of unexpected rent-free space. The Gensler design team also added a set of stairs connecting the executive floors to the original base building as well as two escalators at the ground-floor level to facilitate circulation to the cafeteria on the second floor.

The Gensler planners and designers also upgraded the existing basic building systems. The installation of over 150 miles of IBM Type II cabling was planned, an average of three miles of cabling per typical floor. Gensler oversaw the installation of Enron's IBM/ROLM CBS 9000 telecommunications switch, second only in size in the southwest to the system at NASA, accommodating twelve nodes for a maximum of 5,500 telephones. A data center operations systems center was also installed, along with security cabling and a vertical conveyor to route in-house documents.

Certain fundamental design and space planning concepts formed the basis for the final design of the project. **The overriding concerns involved the client's desire to present an overall sense of unity from one floor to the next. Enron also required a facility that could change and grow according to their specific functional needs.**

Prior to finalizing the design package for the typical office floors, a full-scale, half-floor mock-up was created on site to test and fine-tune all design details, acoustical control, lighting, and furniture systems. As a result of the mock-up, a workplace was created where each of the forty-three typical floors is an efficient and interesting place to work. On all of the elliptical floorplates, the designers installed diagonal white plaster walls which divide the floor into two equal halves. A circulation path runs along the window wall, allowing easy orientation and permitting as much natural light as possible to enter the space. Services such as photocopying, coffee bars, a primary conference room, and mailrooms are located within the special "Z" core that was created from the diagonally placed wall. The designers left windows at column bays open on each end of the floor so that everyone may enjoy the view at various points along the circulation path. Each half of the space is identified by its own color scheme. The designers placed a minimum of three private offices on each end of each floor, with sixty percent of the space in open plan.

The universal layout, recurring from floor to floor, was incorporated by the designers to simplify space management. The universal office concept, innovative at the time, is based upon the idea that all typical offices are a standard size, and open furniture system workstations are of different sizes but share one common dimension, which means that all aisles and power spine locations are pre-set and do not change. This allows various workstations to change length without redrilling floor power outlets to tap power into the electrified furniture system base. This

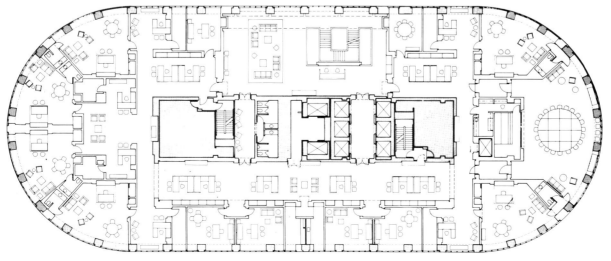

Plans for typical floors show diagonal division and flipped symmetry. Each floor has a minimum of three private offices. Three column bays at each end are always kept open.

strategy improves efficiency of office space and greatly reduces the amount of furniture to be stockpiled for future use, and also simplifies the removal and set up of workstations. **A number of factors – efficient but comfortable space utilization, accommodation of existing architectural elements and workstation options, and the escalating Enron churn rate – suggested that using the universal office concept would be the best design strategy for the Enron facility.**

"The universal office concept has already saved a lot of dollars in reconstruction," says Jim Bernhart, Enron's project officer. "One of the best things that Gensler did was to encourage us to use the universal plan." The Gensler designers initially targeted the Enron churn rate at thirty percent per year; Enron is currently relocating approximately ten percent of the total staff on a monthly basis. By using the universal office concept, Enron can now adapt and fine-tune its operations without costly renovation or disruption of operations. Thanks to the Gensler design, people, not walls, are moved.

In addition to the thoughtful universal layout, Gensler's solution of placing private offices on curved walls adds an unexpected element of artfulness to the interior. Faced with a multitude of offices of different sizes, which Enron inherited in its expansion, **Gensler developed a concept of space where rank would be expressed by furniture and finishing rather than size.**

The Gensler designers located common employee

The 50-story downtown Houston tower designed by Lloyd Jones & Fillpot and developed by Century Development.

The board room ceiling was lowered to 16 feet to create an environment more conducive to meetings. Enron Corp's concern for the human context of business is reflected throughout the headquarters facility.

Horizontal silk fabric panels and a Regency-style cabinet help give a human scale to a 22-foot-high executive reception area.

Chairman's office where Gensler established a strong sense of human scale by incorporating six-foot and four foot, four-inch horizontal sightlines.

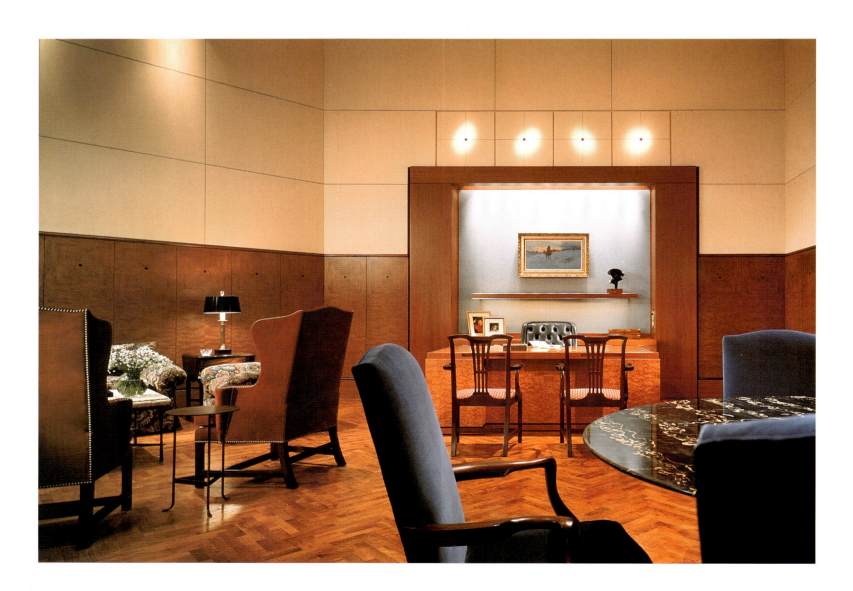

facilities at the heart of this workplace. A colorful, upbeat restaurant called "The Energizer" occupies the entire second floor. Just off the escalators, a dramatic graphic display greets employees and announces the festive atmosphere of the dining facility. A whimsical display of projected colored lights forms the letters of the restaurant's name as they tumble across the entry corridor and lead visitors into the dining area. This facility is located lower in the building to provide diners with a view of the street theater below. The space also hosts two private dining rooms which are available to all employees by reservation for business-related events.

The Gensler team also designed "The Body Shop," a spacious, state-of-the-art fitness center open to all Enron employees, located in the building's basement. The designers created the aerobics area by pushing the exterior wall out. The exposed columns of the building's structural system create an arcade that separates the aerobics area from the nautilus equipment, which forms a rim around the facility.

In addition to the office floors, executive spaces, employee services, and interior graphics for some 1,250,000 square feet of space, the Enron Corp headquarters also includes a gas control area that operates twenty-four hours a day. For this function, the Gensler designers installed operators on a round raised access floor, seated before large screen monitors fitted into the building curve opposite them, as well as individual computers, which enable workers to communicate with field managers.

A special visitor's viewing room was located behind them, with a conference table, which enables others to study activity in the field.

Enron was the largest interior project ever created in Houston, a national landmark of corporate design in its treatment of the general office floor and a textbook example of how to break down corporate hierarchical barriers. Workers' floors rarely hold their own compared to executive quarters in terms of innovation and design equality as they do in this project, which showcases the imaginative possibilities and benefits of universal planning. It was a fast-track project that would not have been possible without Gensler's extensive CAD capability, which has been ahead of the curve of computer-aided design from its inception. The project has won numerous design awards and has become a symbol of Houston's economic power.

Interconnecting stair is designed with two breaks to ensure an easy climb and clear views.

Facing page
Corridor on typical floor. Utilizing a universal plan allows core elements to remain the same on each floor.

Above
Typical open plan and private offices, demonstrating universal plan, where one can move people and not walls.

Typical floor elevator lobby has seating area and makore walls. Reception stations are on lobby and executive floor only.

Previous spread
The Gas Control Group operates 24 hours a day and monitors tens of thousands of miles of pipeline.

"The Energizer" cafeteria features neon and incandescent lighting plus colorful canopy forms. Square motifs, a theme throughout the building, reflect each other from floor and ceiling.

Banquettes in red leather and fabric, reminiscent of the fifties, divide large seating area.

Entry to "The Body Shop" employee gym features colorful lighting signage designed by Gensler.

"The Body Shop" has exercise machines along a paneled curved wall looking into brightly lit aerobics floor.

In 1985, Union Bank of Switzerland (UBS) initially retained Gensler to renovate the bank's existing space at 299 Park Avenue to accommodate immediate functional needs and to plan the expansion of their North American headquarters. **The challenge was to fit the technical needs of this progressive banking organization into a 1967 building that had numerous structural, electrical and mechanical limitations.** In addition, a series of temporary moves orchestrated within the building ultimately provided UBS with contiguous floors conducive to effective staff interaction. The facility features a sophisticated infrastructure that includes raised flooring, two large data centers, and supplemental air conditioning to accommodate the needs of a variety of banking functions. A cafeteria serves up to 2,000 employees and bank customers. Gensler's work on the project eventually evolved into almost 750,000 square feet of planning, design and implementation.

By 1988, a competition to design a private banking space on the street level of the 299 Park Avenue building was heald and the Gensler team won the commission over three Swiss architectural teams. The highly visible, 7,500-square-foot lobby space posed some unusual design challenges. First, Gensler had to create a structure for the imposing 125-foot-long by 25-foot-wide by 24-foot-high space that would fulfill the special requirements of private banking. **Unlike many American banks, the design for Union Bank of Switzerland did not include teller counters, but rather was an environment where the banking officers handled transactions from workstations. The designers also developed waiting areas where private banking clients could be seated comfortably, rather than having to stand in line to be served.** The bank also required a separate area for more complex transactions by investment counselors.

The Gensler designers redefined the existing space into a series of open enclosures, creating what may be described as a series of buildings within a building. Through the introduction of this architectural vocabulary, the vast volume of the street level space was reduced to human scale while simultaneously producing a structural framework for the various functional requirements. The designers executed the building-within-a-building concept by using glass facade-like interior walls with steel and granite portals, which divided the space into separate volumes along the main axis. Gensler suspended a red stainless steel clad structure, formed by a series of 39 arcs supported by two main beams. As it moved through the space, this element created a central axis and formed the semblance of a roof above the created "buildings."

For the entry on Park Avenue, a cylindrical form contains the revolving doors, and the UBS bright red logo color immediately establishes the presence of the banking institution. Through this sculptural entry, one proceeds up the steps, aided by Scott-Burton-designed steel handrails, though a smaller door to the second area and into a 20-foot-high colonnade where

Union Bank of Switzerland

As shown on plan, reception/information desk of granite marks first interior stopping point for visitors who are directed to appropriate transaction stations.

Straight-on view looking up entry stairs to main reception/information desk. designed by Scott Burton. Materials here set continuity for substances throughout the space.

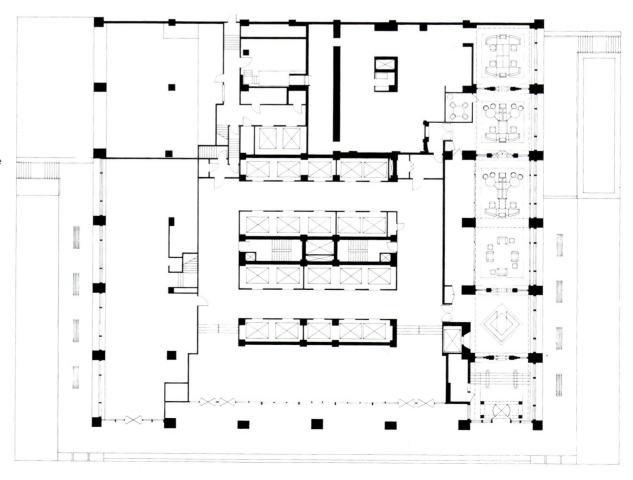

granite columns support an open barrel vault below the ceiling. The colonnade progresses for 125 feet along the window wall, moving from reception to waiting areas, and to the workstations of the investment counselors and financial analysts beyond. Immediately within the shelter of the colonnade, the reception/information desk serves as the location for visitors to be directed through the space to a financial officer.

The next transition break within the progression of space, defined by two bays and wooden screens, leads to the waiting area and transactions section. Off to one side of this space, a gallery space serves as exhibition space for works by Swiss artists living in the United States. Beyond this area, counselors' stations are located for the most private client meetings. The last segment accommodates support staff. Throughout, the design provides employees and visitors alike with dynamic views through the lofty, transparent space to the lively street theater beyond.

Careful attention was given to the choice of materials in an attempt to express the 125-year-old bank's status and stability. Gensler finished this regal space with granite in three finishes. In order to bring the quality of the stainless steel finish up to the level required for this project, the designers used a special electro-polish technique. Gensler then surfaced the walls with perforated leather with insulation backing to control sound and to create a calm atmosphere within the space.

Looking into seating area of main reception area.

The second sector of the banking hall contains waiting area and workstations of two officers, defined by two bays and wooden screens.

Views of two officers' workstations.

Steve Wozniak and Steve Jobs started Apple Computer in April 1976. The young computer engineers' (ages 26 and 21 respectively) first product, a modest, pre-assembled computer circuit board with no keyboard, case, sound, or graphics was created in Steve Jobs' parents' garage. At the time, no one would have imagined that within a few short years they would explode on to the global market and join the ranks of the giants of the computer world. The architects of the first Apple computer positioned themselves not only among other big companies, but ultimately changed the way computers were used around the world. Their pioneering efforts coupled with fresh, youthful ideas helped create personal computers that operated in innovative ways. Apple became synonymous with new approaches. A part of the success of their products can be clearly attributed to the high quality of the simple design principles they adhered to. Their "user friendly" philosophy, together with an instinct for innovation and good design, extended to the development of their facilities. Apple's collaboration with architects, interior designers, and planners was informed by the company's need to translate and fine tune its image into successful workplace design.

When the Gensler team began working with Apple, they quickly realized that Apple would be a demanding client, but also that their clear focus and commitment would carry the design process to the best possible results. **Apple's solid corporate identity was expressed clearly, as was their appreciation for quality design. Apple understood the importance of the work environment and how those spaces could reinforce their corporate culture.** John Sculley, former Chairman and CEO at Apple, expressed the desire that each of Apple's buildings would have its own specific identity and hoped that the design would extend this appreciation of individuality to the users. The Gensler designers established a distinct design vocabulary for each facility while maintaining a level of continuity in furniture systems so that each facility could be easily managed. The individual identity of each facility was achieved by focusing the design effort on common areas.

In order to understand the company's various needs, Gensler had to penetrate Apple's corporate culture before work could begin on the facilities. Gensler found this highly dynamic, rapidly growing company to be sensitive to providing its employees with informal environments that foster individual creativity. At the De Anza 3 and the Research and Development facilities, for example, the designers found that employees were most comfortable in a casual environment. Apple has open hours and employees often work late; spaces had to perform not simply from nine-to-five, but on a twenty-four hour schedule. Apple's United States Customer Service Center, where computer experts talk customers through their various computer problems, is a unique space. Although this facility was conceived as an inexpensive space with a short-term lease, the designers still had to establish an environment

Apple Computer, Inc.

Apple Computer, Inc.
De Anza 3
Corridor between window wall overlooking courtyard outside and workstations within.

Three-level elevation of the building, seen from the courtyard.

that would foster creative energy. The project for Apple's Research and Development facility provided the Gensler designers with the opportunity to experiment with innovative ways of organizing the workplace, and their work for Apple's Market Center provided the company with its most public face, presenting the business world with an image of a mature Apple. The common denominator is the energy and "Apple spirit" which is present in all the facilities. As Apple grew, the Gensler designers continued to interpret their position and create facilities that not only reflected where Apple was but where they were going.

Apple Computer, Inc.
De Anza 3
Architectural device used as a screen to hide the sea of workstations. View is into workstations on one side and into the atrium on the other.

Apple Computer, Inc.
De Anza 3
Another corridor, with hub formation at right.

The renovation of the De Anza 3 facility (the name refers to the street and number) at Apple Computer's property in Cupertino, California, was a significant part of Gensler's ongoing relationship with Apple. The building, originally constructed in 1980, sustained damage in an October 1989 earthquake, necessitating total renovation.

Gensler planned and designed the interiors of the new facility which accommodates 533 open workstations, fifty-seven private offices, computer laboratories, a cafeteria, and an auditorium and conference center. The facility was planned for the Network Division, who wished to have all cabling fully accessible for quick, temporary installations within a highly flexible, universal floor plan. **Gensler's task for this four-story building, with vast 53,000-square-foot floorplates, was to provide the 600-plus Apple employees occupying the space with the kind of informal working environment to which Apple is committed.**

This space was designed for Apple's Networking and Communications group, whose task it is to advance the technology for modems, laser printers, and scanners. **The overriding concern was the inclusion of exposed cable trays to accommodate the extensive wiring required to distribute cable to all offices and laboratory areas.** In order to meet technology requirements, the Gensler designers called for two of these easily accessible cable trays, one floating above a low perforated wall, and a supplementary cabling system (developed by Gensler in collaboration with Herman Miller) closer at hand. This supplementary cabling system allows for more immediate access. Seated employees can simply connect to individual machines without assistance. Both systems were incorporated to allow for the frequent redistribution of cables used for testing machines that the users of this facility are constantly working with.

In addition to the open work areas and laboratory spaces on each of the upper floors, a series of circular hubs are positioned between the interior courtyard and the exterior window wall along an imaginary diagonal. These hubs were designed to contain shared facilities such as coffee rooms, copy machines, conference and meeting rooms, as well as storage and communications areas. These circular hubs are focal points of the design vocabulary and are used to identify major points of entry within the space. The hubs also help to create a sense of community within the workplace as they function as both important resource centers and social meeting spaces for the employees. The cruciform pattern is partially repeated on the ground floor, where two angular enclosures shelter work space and, diagonally across, a small sector of the employee cafeteria. All the systems furniture in the space follow Apple's standards. They are positioned within a universal plan for the facility so that workstations need not be reconfigured, thereby alleviating costly rewiring.

The Gensler team organized the interior spaces around the central courtyard. Interior windows look

Apple Computer, Inc., De Anza 3

Apple Computer, Inc.
De Anza 3
The Networking and Communications Group is located in an existing building with large floorplates. The building surrounds an open courtyard.

Cafeteria, looking toward servery and behind curved hub enclosure to more private dining space. Carpet pattern repeats light-wave motif.

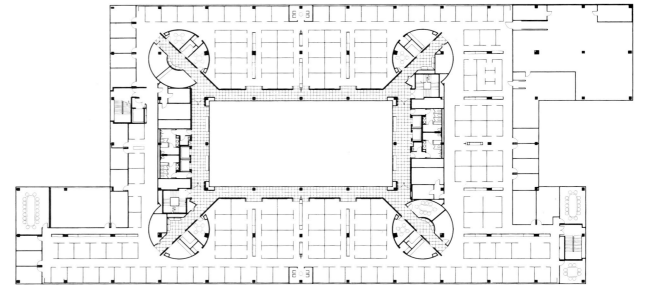

Apple Computer, Inc.
De Anza 3
Full view of the reception area, introducing variations on the light-wave theme used throughout the facility.

on to the courtyard where the primary circulation routes are located. The designers relied on the window walls to form the exterior wall of the corridors, and to provide the interior trafficked areas around the courtyard with both views and light, and textured plaster walls in two shades of apricot were used to form the interior boundary. The circulation path is clearly defined around the courtyard by the incorporation of custom patterned carpeting colored for each floor.

The Gensler team established a design vocabulary for the interiors based on a visual translation of the technology's communications medium, specifically light waves. The notion of light waves is suggested by the undulating divider wall edges, reception desk detailing, and carpet patterns. In keeping with the inventive, creative spirit of the facility, the designers then focused their choice of finish colors on electric blue, red, and turquoise, with different hues deployed to code-carpeted circulation routes on each floor. For the sake of economy, the Gensler designers made creative use of inexpensive materials throughout the facility.

In order to allow light into the interior spaces, the designers punctured the apricot-colored plaster walls with square window-like openings. Although they provide both visual and acoustic privacy for the changing combinations of workstations and offices located beyond, these walls introduce the idea of layering, and unexpected vistas are found throughout the entire project.

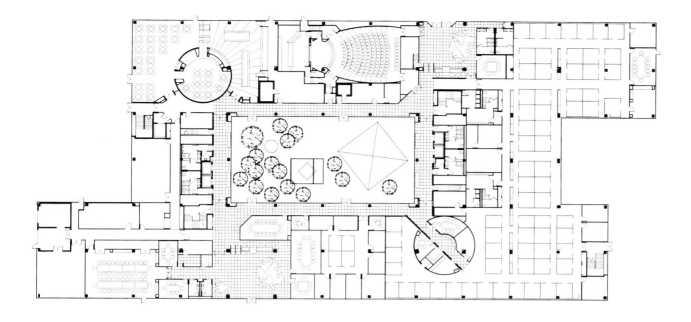

Apple Computer, Inc.
De Anza 3
Detail of cable tray that ties into Herman Miller panel systems.

Workstation partitions showing client-mandated presence of exposed cable trays high above desks.

Apple's Research and Development campus in Cupertino, California consists of five four-story buildings designated for office use and a two-story structure which accommodates dining, library, and auditorium facilities around a secured courtyard. Within the courtyard the base building architects included an amphitheater and various sport courts. The Gensler team of designers provided interior architectural design for Building 1, the main point of entry for the entire campus. In addition to the office facilities, this building was designed to host an Apple products retail store, conference and video conference rooms, classrooms, software library, and other common areas on the first floor, as well as a staff cafe that enlivens the ground level of the four-story atrium.

Gensler was asked to create a facility that could consolidate parts of Apple's research and development facilities already located in various parts of Silicon Valley. **Apple's primary goal for the new facility was to provide a collaborative work atmosphere for their Research and Development engineers that would foster individual creativity and improve the "time to market" for new products.** The environment reflects the Apple spirit, as its setting is casual and functional.

Building 1, which was designed for the Advanced Products and Advanced Technology Groups, incorporates a four-story atrium at the center of the 50,000-square-foot floorplates. The interesting structure presented a unique challenge for the Gensler designers. Though it brought natural light and air into the center of vast floorplates, the atrium created two somewhat disconnected wings. The Gensler designers united the spaces visually by tying the bridge through the atrium to the two thoroughfares, or internal "Main Streets," on each side of the building. The designers used this thoroughfare as an organizing element within the space to orient users to the side corridors, each of which terminates in natural light at the window wall. Circulation is assisted by incorporating four accent walls into the design vocabulary, each coded in rich colors to identify various sectors of the various floors.

Two important types of user-defined common areas are located along the "Main Street" axis, and these spaces are at the center of the innovative strategy of the facility in general. Previously, the design for Apple's work spaces consisted of large, open plan environments with clusters of workstations and a few private offices flanked by support areas. After assessing Apple's many facilities and attempting to project their needs for this space into the future, **Gensler worked with Apple's design team to develop a new way of organizing the Apple workspace by developing a planning concept based on the creation of a series of small suite-type groupings.** These groupings are each composed of approximately twelve to fifteen staff members, positioned primarily in private offices, which are clustered around an open common area. In addition to the cluster of private offices, area associates are positioned in nearby open workstations

Apple Computer, Inc. Research & Development

Apple Computer, Inc. Research & Development. The planning approach — a series of smaller suite-type groupings with staff in private offices — represents a new way of thinking for Apple.

Looking from inside coffee bar to User Defined Area.

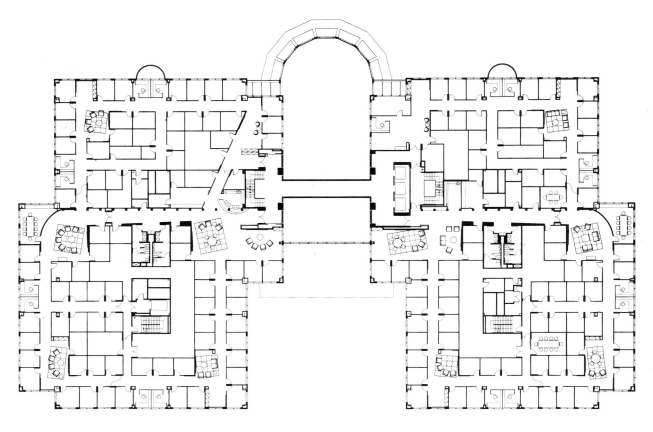

One of the larger User Defined Areas, which are strategically located around the building. Employees can meet and gather in these spaces.

Apple Computer, Inc. Research & Development. User Defined Area in one of the neighborhoods which comprise the building. Each group of engineers has its own User Defined Area.

at, or adjacent to, the windows. The common areas were designed to include filing and storage, a laser printer, or other office equipment, conference areas, lounge, or even additional workstations if necessary. The Gensler designers created flexible spaces which became identified as User Defined Areas for each of the clusters of staff members in order to convey a sense of individual empowerment, and as the use of these areas is at the discretion of the group, a sense of community. **In fact, the most unique aspect of the design solution for this facility is the extensive use of such User Defined Areas. Designed to encourage communication and the exchange of ideas, these areas are ready to be adapted by the users to meet their needs.** Furnished with adjustable lighting, furniture on casters, provisions for printers, faxes, and video monitors and full-height white boards, the spaces are highly flexible. Common support functions are located along the central "spine/main street," which has a vaulted ceiling and asymmetrical architecture to help differentiate the two sides of the floor.

The entire facility seems to create a balance between public and private spaces, and the designers often differentiate these types of spaces, with the use of color and materials.

Apple Computer, Inc. Research & Development. User Defined Area in major hub of building. Open coffee bar is the structure on right.

One of the few enclosed administrative workstations in the facility. Some amenities include adjustable lighting, furniture on casters, provision for printers, faxes, and video monitors.

Private offices are clustered around an open common area to enhance collaboration and communication.

Apple Computer, Inc. Research & Development. Product display area of the Company Store is located in Apple Computer, Inc. Research & Development facility.

Apple Computer, Inc. Research & Development. Company Store combines display, information area, and workstations.

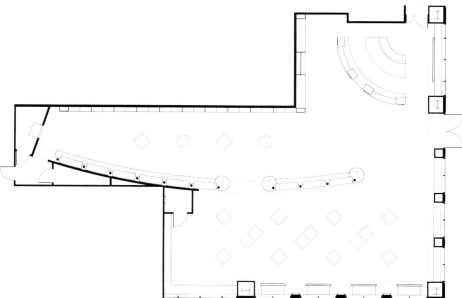

Apple Computer, Inc.
Research & Development.
Detail of one of the steel supports which holds the computer display.

Detail of the cash-wrap area.

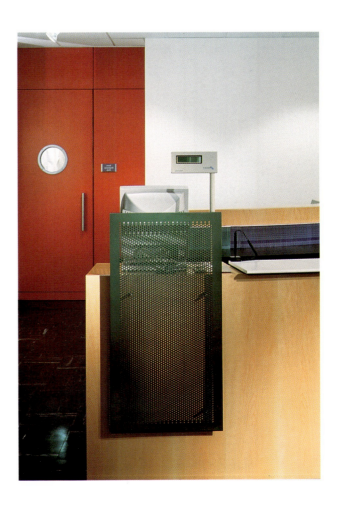

Apple's facility in Austin, Texas was designed to accommodate the company's user support center for the United States, as well as all accounting and payroll functions. Gensler collaborated with The Bommorito Group of Austin on the project which involved the renovation of two industrial buildings. (Gensler also provided conceptual graphic design on the project.) **Apple consolidated several customer support divisions into this facility, bringing together groups that were once spread across the country.** The project represents the success of Gensler's involvement in partnering, demonstrating how Gensler can join hands with client, contractor, local design firm, and furniture dealer to create a team capable of completing the project on an aggressive schedule and very limited budget.

Within the void of this former industrial space, the design team had to create a workplace environment that would provide both open vistas and local scale that served both the technical needs of the telephone- and computer-intensive work, and that provided the staff with an interesting and varied work space. The designers were on the tightest of schedules and had to direct their choices to meet a demanding construction budget without compromising the aesthetics of the interiors. Working within a five-month schedule from conceptual design to move-in, the design team was able to create a highly unique space in a limited time.

The design team took full advantage of the industrial nature of the selected buildings, with their dramatic ceiling heights and uncommon opportunities, to create a dynamic workspace. Following the model provided by the naturally large, open spaces of the Texas landscape, the planning concept for the interior spaces is based on the idea of an imaginary river.

The designers established a "river" that "flows" from building to building, connected by means of open walkways. The imaginary current continues through the various spaces, where built-out areas are shaped or skewed in plan, as if pushed there by the random force of the "river." Sloping walls run along the hallways and seem to form "canyons" cut into the space by the (metaphorical) flow of water. Even the reflected ceiling plan has been incorporated into the narrative scheme to become a "sky" above the built landscape below. Taking advantage of the height of the space, an open ceiling grid was positioned to hover above and host "clouds," which are actually geometric arrangements of rectilinear acoustical ceiling tiles.

The Gensler designers invested simple materials with a visual energy that becomes part of the entire project. Gypsum board boxes were built at different heights to act as navigational devices in the vast space. Varied shapes and intense colors are used on the walls and for the carpets to enliven the space where diverse planes meet. These interventions provide major way-finding landmarks; for example, large, free-standing coral-colored cubes house the rest rooms and become important geometric elements within the visual composition that helps define this workplace landscape.

Apple Computer, Inc.
U.S. Customer Service Center

Apple Computer, Inc.
U.S. Customer Service Center
Custom reception desk fronts canted wall with white-on-white Apple logo.

Corridor with aligned work centers are arranged to provide interaction among a variety of divisional staffs.

Apple Computer, Inc.
U.S. Customer Service Center
One of two sculpturesque high-back chairs and red-defined telephone booths.

Typical workstation area.

Apple Computer, Inc.
U.S. Customer Service Center
Closed and open entries to conference space and restrooms; informal break area in rear leads to cafeteria.

Workstation detail.

Becton Dickinson approached Gensler in 1990 to evaluate the programmatic needs of their Immunocytometry Systems Division. This division, which manufactures highly sophisticated cell sorting equipment, was seeking to consolidate in a single facility several departments that had been previously located in four separate buildings. Becton Dickinson's goal was to facilitate interdepartmental communications. They needed a facility capable of housing activities ranging from state-of-the-art laboratories that would meet stringent FDA guidelines, to manufacturing areas, warehouse space, and offices for researchers, technicians, and administrators. In addition to these facilities, Becton Dickinson wanted to incorporate amenities that would create a unified workplace and establish a sense of community among company employees.

An existing 235,000-square-foot building (a former electronics production facility) was purchased by Becton Dickinson, and a detailed space program was developed by Gensler as well as space utilization studies. The Gensler team was asked to create a design that would unify and humanize the space while establishing an environment that would speak of quality and permanence.

Major modifications to the existing steel-framed building were made to accommodate Becton Dickinson's requirements. The Gensler designers modified the building's skin to allow for the incorporation of windows and skylights in newly created office areas. With the addition of three thirty-foot square skylights, for example, the designers were able to transform what had previously been a large internal manufacturing area into a light-filled office space. **The Gensler designers created equity across departments in the new offices, incorporating one common workstation size and one private office size to maintain consistency among the various departments and provide a framework for future flexibility.** The extensive natural light allowed into the space combined with a soft color palette reinforces the simplicity of the architecture and continues to open up the office areas visually which is a welcome contrast for much of the technical staff, who necessarily spend a great deal of time in closed laboratories and clean-rooms (air controlled spaces). Great attention was paid to the design and planning of the facilities' extensive mechanical services and to the creation of properly scaled, simple interior spaces.

A prominent, new two-story semicircular structure was designed to create a new entry to the facility. It provides a dramatic reception area, and creates a unified visual transition between the two main parts of the building structure. The total program for the facility required that construction be phased over a period of 18 months. Gensler created nearly 20,000 square feet for manufacturing; 100,000 square feet for research and development, laboratories, and clean-rooms; and 100,000 square feet for office spaces. In addition, employee amenities such as a cafeteria located in the atrium garden, a fitness

Becton Dickinson
Immunocytometry Systems

An existing structure, a former electronics production facility, was transformed into an efficient research and office facility.

Facing page
Interior atrium features landscaping supports, 14 feet at their highest and gradually decreasing in size, ending up at four-foot six inch level.

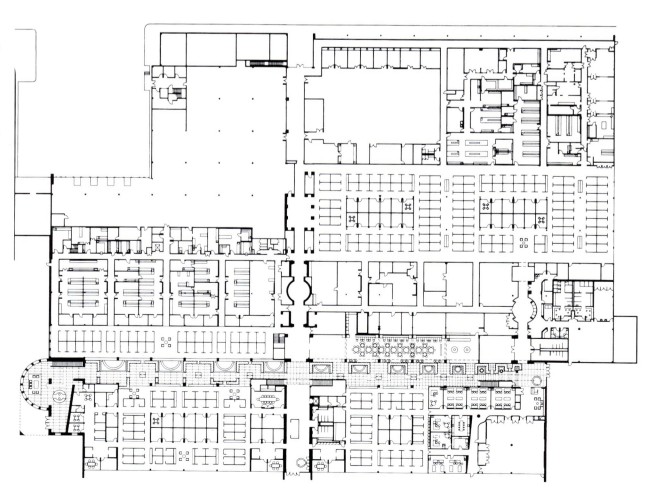

center, and a training center were incorporated into the design plan.

The focal point of this project became a very large interior atrium designed to function as a common area for informal meetings, cafeteria space, and the primary entrance to the research, manufacturing, and office blocks. The twenty-five-foot wide, 474-foot long atrium space was redesigned to not only connect the various parts of the facility, but also to provide a frame of reference for orientation and a physical "heart" for the workplace community. The Gensler designers referred to the individual departments as working neighborhoods, connecting them with the street-like space of the atrium. An interior garden was established along the length of the atrium and landscaped with a series of reflecting pools and formal, U-shaped green structures that help define intimate meeting and dining areas within the space. Christine Banks, one of the principal Gensler designers on the project, explained that the intention was to create a design device that did not immediately reveal itself for what it was. She and the Gensler team were hoping to create a series of structures that looked entirely different when viewed from the balcony than when seen at eye level. To address this complex challenge the talents of landscape designer Martha Schwartz were employed.

The issue, as Ms. Schwartz recalls, was to use garden elements to create distinct areas within the long, narrow space. Working with the Gensler designers she created a series of rectilinear, sculptural hedge supports. The areas where the hedge supports rise highest were intended for informal conferences, which can be held in the sheltered privacy of the tall U-shaped structures; the shorter structures are in place in the cafeteria dining area, for example, where open views are more desirable. Sanseveria was used in the raised planters surrounded by pools. The simple plant, while classified as a house plant, is cited by NASA and Associated Landscape Contractors of America as capable of removing up to seventy percent of indoor air pollutants. The plant and the structures were also chosen since vines clinging to armatures obviate the need for pruning, keeping maintenance to a minimum. At the time of completion, it was estimated that the structures would be covered with growth in approximately seven years. The gradual growth of the plants provided continual interest for employees who kept an eye on the progress of the plants as if they were in their own gardens.

The green structures were also interspersed with fountains, pools, and planters. The sound of the flowing water functions as white noise, muting the acoustics of voices and footsteps within the large, open space. In order to reinforce the central axis of the space, a colonnade of palm trees was incorporated as well. Becton Dickinson technicians, seeking a break from the confinement of labs and research rooms, particularly welcome the sunny diversion this space provides.

Building exterior at entry. Gensler's most important objective was to unify the three existing steel-framed buildings and the connecting atrium.

Lobby view from stairs. A new double-height semicircular reception area provides visual transition between the two main units.

Open office environment houses engineering staff. A 30,000-square-foot second level was added atop a warehouse, for use as a research and development facility.

Atrium with view into employee cafeteria. The atrium serves as the building's primary connector, and when combined with the landscaping elements, looks entirely different when seen from the balcony and when seen at eye level.

Corridor looking into manufacturing unit. Each departmental sector required different design and construction.

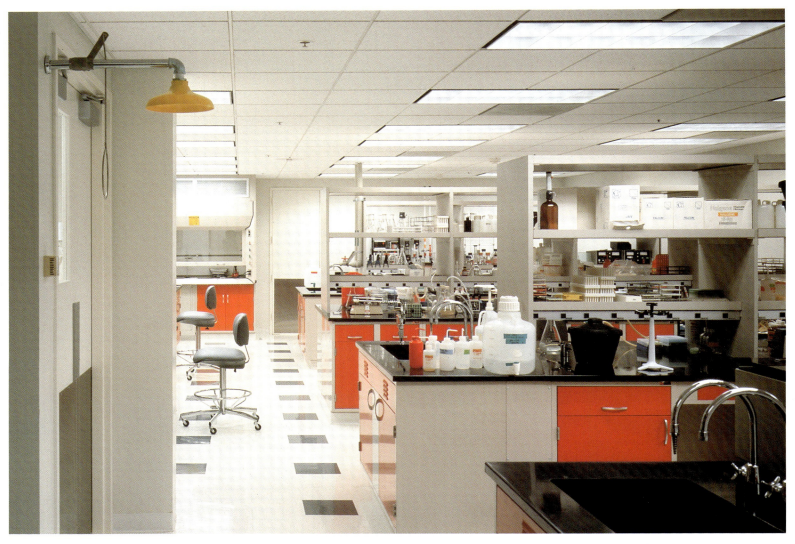

Laboratory space is part of 100,000-square-foot air-controlled area dedicated to research and development, labs and clean rooms.

Executive conference room is visually accessible to passers-by.

Office space housing research and development group.

Open office for manufacturing support. Providing visual unity are light colors, clear and frosted glass, white perforated metal, and vivid accent carpeting.

Epson America, Inc., a U.S. affiliate of Japan-based Seiko Epson Corporation, a global technology company, expanded its business operations in the Americas during the 1980s. At the time, their customer service, sales, marketing, and finance groups were located in six separate buildings within a two-square mile area in Torrance, California. With the goal of consolidating operations in a new state-of-the-art facility that would reflect the organization's corporate image, Epson purchased a 10.5-acre parcel directly adjacent to the Civic Center in Torrance and sponsored a design competition for the new headquarters. Adhering to terms set forth in the property's existing conditional use permit, as well as addressing Epson's specialized criteria, Gensler won the competition with its design of a low-rise complex that would appear as four separate buildings from the street, yet internally would function in a unified fashion. An important Epson consideration was that the building allow for the greatest flexibility as they intended to mesh their own technology products – printers, computers, and scanners – with the building system's automation and wire management. **Epson required a building that would allow their organization to quickly respond to a dynamic industry and office automation trends worldwide.** In addition to these functional requirements, Epson America desired a building that would address their Japanese origins while simultaneously blending with the California surroundings. **Epson was particularly concerned with energy conservation issues, with very direct goals of low power consumption through system design as well as passive solar design.**

Completed in the fall of 1990, the new Epson America corporate headquarters makes every effort to combine an energy-conserving design with a strong use of natural and raw materials. The Gensler team sought to use basic Japanese principles of design without directly referencing Japanese architecture. In order to do so, they incorporated natural wood, unadorned metals, and exposed concrete, paying careful attention to proportion and scale. The use of clear glass, rather than a conventional energy-conserving reflective glass, creates a totally transparent barrier between the building's interior and the garden outside, made possible by the use of passive solar shading of windows. For the site, the Gensler architects and designers created a four-building complex around a garden accessible from the inside, with secured entry points at each of the four corners of the quadrangle. Through this arrangement of the basic architectural elements, the Gensler team created a design vocabulary grounded in simple, straight lines and flat planes. Each building maintains its own identifiable secured entrance to facilitate an exit strategy while retaining the uniform composition of the entire complex if Epson should ever choose to lease portions of the building. The Gensler architects also rotated the structures of the complex to maximize perimeter views over garden spaces which screen parking.

Epson America, Inc.

Page 106
Exterior of front of building, showing entrance canopy. With little ornamentation, the buildings rely on proportion for their beauty.

Page 107
View into main reception lobby from across driveway. Gensler's design wraps from the exterior to the interiors, unifying the outside and interior in a seamless whole.

Anchoring the predominant corner of the four-building site is a three-story executive building with atrium topped by large pyramidal skylight.

The Epson facility was built to support and cultivate staff innovation and quick response to market shifts. Passive solar shading devices keep direct sunlight out of office space near windows while reflecting light deeply into interior spaces.

Anchoring the main corner of the site is a three-story executive building with an atrium topped by a large pyramidal skylight. This building houses executive offices and board rooms, in addition to conference rooms, reception, and training rooms. Designed to be suffused by reflected and filtered natural light, its luminous quality is remarkable and energy-efficient, as lights are designed to automatically turn off when natural light levels are sufficient for work. Across the garden, the executive building is balanced by another three-story building that hosts service-oriented facilities which are sheltered from view. Closing the sides of the garden court between these structures are two additional two-story structures.

In order to meet the design requirements, the two-story structures were designed to accommodate a wide variety of functions, from laboratories to general office areas. They are highly flexible and consist almost entirely of open offices. To offset the vastness of these spaces, the designers placed the ceiling height at ten feet. **In a setting where frequent rearrangements of multiple workstations can become difficult and costly, the effective solution was to provide forty-foot by forty-foot column bays for unlimited adaptability of space.** Epson decided early on that an access floor would be required in approximately eighty percent of the facility. Because of the nature of their workplace, wire management required the flexibility that an access floor provides. Circulating under the access floor is also conditioned air with several small registers located in each of the workspaces so that individuals can regulate the amount of air to suit their needs. While popular in England, Germany, and South Africa, at the time, **Epson's headquarters represented the first large-scale application of under-floor air delivery in the United States. The result has been extraordinary, with no air-quality complaints registered, and a significant energy reduction compared with conventionally air-conditioned buildings.** Removable walls were also incorporated in all enclosed spaces (except the building core) creating completely open floor plans that could be redesigned with minimal construction dust or debris. The Gensler team provided Epson America with a space that can shift easily from offices into a laboratory area, or meeting rooms from high to low density without ever changing a mixing box or a duct.

For the exterior design the Gensler architects employed natural daylighting concepts to reduce both artificial illumination and heat absorption. A key component to enhancing available light while simultaneously reducing solar heat and minimizing the need for artificial illumination and its own radiant heat can be found just outside the building's deeply recessed windows. The architects attached four-foot, six-inch deep aluminum "light shelves" that project one foot beyond the precast building skin; these are mounted on struts outside each window. The flat bottom surfaces of these horizontal shading devices are eight feet above the level of the finished floor and run parallel to it. The shelves protect the interior against excessive absorption of heat, and by reflecting light into the space, allow perimeter light fixtures to be turned off during the day if desired. The curved high-gloss upper surface of the shelf is calibrated to reflect daylight through the upper two feet of the windows and back into the high ceilings, which diffuse it throughout the space; the skylights also diffuse the illumination of the atria. These devices are designed to conserve energy required for lighting while creating a sense of translucence and serenity characteristic throughout the building.

The Gensler team structured circulation patterns in the buildings to route employees and visitors around the courtyard in order to reach other areas. All the buildings creating the court are knitted together by a corridor loop, which makes travel around each 80,000-square-foot floor compact and intuitive. The circulation system is a flexible arrangement of conventional double-loaded corridor offices or a single-loaded open space planning layout that does not sacrifice desirable lease depths and keeps major traffic away from work areas.

The Gensler team worked with Takeo Uesugi & Associates to create a Japanese-inspired park-like setting in the interior courtyard space. The foliage, rock formations, and running water provide a dramatic visual backdrop that contributes color and natural variation to every room overlooking the courtyard, and offer a pleasant place of retreat for the building's users.

For this project, the Gensler architects, planners, and designers won the 1990 Design for Excellence Award from the California Energy Commission and Southern California Edison for an energy-saving system, and a Special Recognition Award from the American Institute of Architects/Cabrillo Chapter.

Closer view of interior entry node from courtyard (curved blade). The corners, or entry nodes, join the buildings as glass-enclosed, two-story breezeways.

Page 111
Dusk shot of node blade between buildings. The nodes serve as emergency exits, house elevators and control vertical circulation.

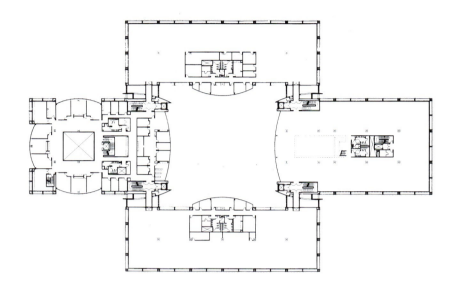

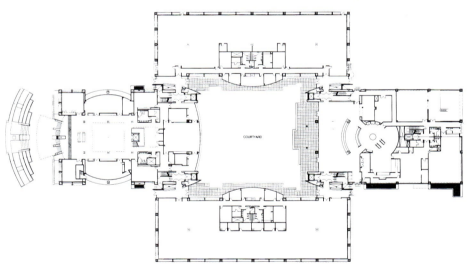

Entry nodes give staff easy access to the circulation corridor that links the four buildings, with views of the landscaped courtyard.

Second Floor Plan.
With a wide open floor plan, maximum space efficiencies are achieved.

First Floor Plan.
To inject a sense of quality throughout the four buildings, Gensler varied the proportion and volume of interior spaces.

Employee dining area, and computer center, can be found on different levels in the rear building of the complex.

Upgraded carpeting and new furniture give the space a refined, yet not lavish, look. Those finishes were carried over into highly trafficked areas in the other buildings.

Main atrium from center of second floor showing elevators.

Previous page
Back atrium toward elevator core.

First floor detail of stair leading to executive area.

Fully-equipped training center provides a comfortable learning environment for trainees.

Individual workstations feature raised access flooring. Individual panels make this floor as steady underfoot as a concrete slab, and wire management plans and underfloor air delivery make new workstation configurations relatively simple.

Taylor + Smith

The Houston-based advertising firm of Taylor + Smith approached Gensler with its plan to create an office unlike any other. **The firm wanted a space that would be functional while engaging people creatively and challenging preconceived notions of what makes a successful workplace, as well as what makes for a successful advertising campaign.** The project was to embody the principles that the firm's president, Larry Taylor, espoused in his dictum, "Be an orange." The central idea of this philosophy is to overcome "apple-thinking," or conventional ideas, which often lead to mediocrity. Taylor hoped for a space that would prepare employees and clients alike to be receptive to new ideas and generate fresh solutions. He wanted the design to underscore the importance of choice and believed that creativity is born of adversity, and that people do their best work when their environment is slightly out of control.

The Gensler design team accepted Taylor's proposition and went about designing a space where creative ideas could be presented, and more importantly, a space that would communicate notions of creativity, diversity, and that would mirror the often chaotic visual world in which we live. The designers did not embrace chaos for chaos' sake though; rather, they created an environment that plays with the unexpected and challenges people to be more productive and responsive to new proposals. Gensler's interior architecture set the stage for general creativity through features that were physically and symbolically significant to the tasks of forming and receiving ideas. The agency was divided into two functionally separate zones: one where clients and prospective clients are received, and a second area in which the creative and production work of the agency is done. This second space required room for both private work and employee interaction. All activity was to take place in an environment that stimulated employees to seek fresh approaches to their clients' advertising needs.

Upon entering the Taylor + Smith space one is immediately impressed by its unique appearance. The entry corridor seems dark and unfinished with its open-grid ceiling and mottled cement floor. This area is intended to encourage visitors to abandon their preconceptions about what an advertising agency is and how it should look. At the end of the Kafkaesque corridor, the visitor is greeted by a receptionist seated behind a giant yellow #2 pencil, some twenty feet long and perfectly scaled, into which the designers have built a desk and reception center. To add to the theatrics of the space, a "Freudian chair," a sculpture closely resembling a chair that cannot seat anyone, has been placed before the reception area/pencil.

The corridor is intended to provoke a sense of unease, but in the reception seating area, referred to as "Grandma's living room," the goal was to reinforce the notion of choice. The designers created five identically styled, custom-designed, overstuffed armchairs for the space. As if in some hallucinogenic version of the childhood tale of Goldilocks and the Three Bears, each of the chairs is a different size, and the visitor is forced to make a decision about which

View from window wall with view toward elevators. Giant pencil sculpture is on one side with reception area on the other. Purpose: to jolt clients and staff into open mindedness.

The entry corridor appears to be unfinished, with an open-grid ceiling and speckled cement floor. The wall is plumb on one end and gradually tilts 30 degrees at the other.

In the seating area, visitors are invited to choose which of the five different-sized, overstuffed chairs is just right.

On the way to the presentation theater, one must cross a bridge. Monitors project whatever mood Taylor + Smith wants to set.

chair is right for him or her. Next to the table, a large framed painting is propped up against the wall. The painting attempts to break down ideas of representation by continuing the image outside of the frame and onto the wall, and by incorporating "real" bud vases into the total image.

The space appears as if in a state of metamorphosis in order to establish a metaphor for the generation of ideas and creative patterns. The designers installed a visually complex bridge that carries visitors to the presentation theater and creates an expectation of what is to come. Shifting images from a bank of nine video monitors constantly wash the bridge in light. In addition to projecting advertising spots produced by the agency, the monitors flash images that convey whatever mood Taylor + Smith wants to set for their clients. For example, the monitors might show a seascape, a forest, or rock concert depending on the atmosphere desired.

The theater was designed to provide a perfect forum for multi-media presentations. Positioned opposite the leaning wall, it opens wide to provide occupants with a sweeping feeling. Within the space, various lighting zones are incorporated and only the necessary parts of the room are darkened, keeping viewers' attention focused on the presentation. There is a custom-designed fiberboard and steel conference table in the shape of a circle with two wings which can be disassembled into smaller tables of varied shapes and sizes and an adjustable credenza. Unlike many corporate conference rooms where the equipment needed for meetings is hidden behind screens, all the facilities at Taylor + Smith are clearly within view and easily accessible. The walls are covered with tackable mohair to convey the notion that this is a working room.

For the employees of Taylor + Smith, the designers established a "Town Hall" which provides a break from the workday and a place "where anything might happen." **The design allows people to escape from the corporate structure and to step out of the established framework.** Employees may eat meals, have informal conversations, punch a bag, or shoot hoops there.

Following Taylor + Smith's specifications, the Gensler team created a series of thirty-three individual work spaces designed for both privacy and interaction. These spaces, referred to as "Home Bases," are raw, experimental, and laboratory-like, and occupants are encouraged to personalize their space. These areas are carpeted, in contrast to all other building spaces which have stained concrete flooring. It was important to Taylor + Smith that employees be able to choose what to do within their own space. Workers were given the components, but they put the elements together according to their own desires. **Personalizing one's own territory is an important expression of the philosophy of the individual that presides at the agency.** In response to this notion, the designers felt it was important not to create a "total picture" but to leave some elements open to individual interpretation. Although almost all employees occupy these workspaces, less than fifty percent of each person's time is spent in these havens. The designers were required, therefore, to incorporate various conference rooms for group work and informal meetings into the overall interior plan.

The Gensler design team used this project as a proving ground for showing what design-on-a-budget could accomplish. For example, the Gensler team searched resale shops and antique stores, and purchased twenty Knoll Pollock conference room chairs at considerable savings. The designers also kept the finishes simple and inexpensive, while still meeting the client's requirement of producing a creative, functional space.

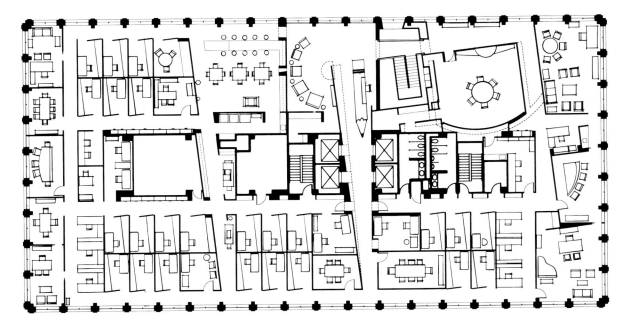

The plan emphasizes private spaces for quiet work and numerous interaction areas.

Personalized "Home Bases" are the domain of users, who may configure the furnishings and decorate the space anyway they wish.

Corridor of "Home Bases" shows how the office environment resembles a small village.

The theater is on the opposite side of the tumbling wall; it opens wide and gives an uplifting feeling.

"Town Hall" employee break area is a place where people escape from corporate structure or work their way out of a creative block.

In 1986, Gensler was retained by Davis Polk & Wardwell to assist the company in evaluating potential office locations that would accommodate future growth. Gensler analyzed the law firm's existing offices as well as five other buildings in Manhattan in terms of optimal location, planning, design, and cost. Based on these studies, the ideal core, footprint, and other requirements such as elevator service, structural reinforcement, conveyor system, and security were determined. In 1988, Davis Polk & Wardwell entered into a twenty-year lease on sixteen floors that were then under construction above the Grand Central Terminal Post Office in Manhattan.

While the building was still on the drawing board, Gensler communicated Davis Polk & Wardwell's complex technical and programming requirements to the building architects and developers. This early involvement was fortuitous because the initial design for the space had significant impact on the final building footprint, and several important structural elements were included as part of the base building and were executed at the landlord/developer's expense: an internal shaft for their conveyor system, specially programmed elevator service to crossover floors, structural reinforcement of the building slab for high density areas for filing and a library, and high ceilings for the spaces intended as cafeteria and conference center. The floorplate sizes easily met the minimum requirement for the 500-attorney Davis Polk & Wardwell New York practice.

With input from their client, the designers established two main criteria: all partner offices would be fifteen by fifteen feet and all associate offices would be ten by fifteen feet. This would enable future double occupancy of all associate size offices. The mix of associate offices and their locations would be compatible with the ratio of offices required for partners.

The firm required a design that would allow it to meet its goal of creating an integrated, expandable workplace. The Gensler designers placed at least one conference room at the perimeter of the floorplan. Other internal space would be used for conference rooms, legal assistants' work areas, case rooms, and specialized libraries. The plan called for all floors to be serviced by a mail conveyor and centralized coffee and copy stations. The designers saw the need for an internal stairway to ease circulation for the many attorneys, staff, and clients in the busy office.

Davis Polk & Wardwell approached Gensler with a clear sense of firm identity as well as functional needs. **The firm takes great pride in its quality work and professional staff, as well as its office environment, and the Gensler designers set about to reflect this spirit in the finished project of their office interiors.** The space was planned in response to the functional needs of the law firm, while simultaneously expressing the firm's desire for a classical yet contemporary space that would convey a subtle, solid image to clients. The designers decided to treat the practice group areas and support areas equally, and both areas

Davis Polk & Wardwell

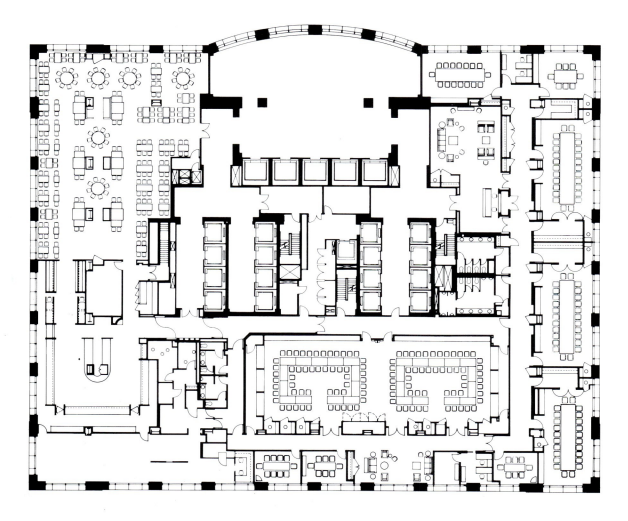

Gensler developed a critical planning dimension and using that input, the architects created a shorter building and a fatter floorplate, which maximized the efficiency of space per partner on a typical floor.

Eighth floor reception area which sets the tone that conveys the appropriate corporate culture.

A blend of modern furniture and traditional materials in the reception area.

received a great deal of thought and planning.

The Gensler team established a design vocabulary based on the subtle symmetry of a square grid and combined this vocabulary with careful detailing. The geometry of the square and rectangle was established as the prevailing formal foundation of the design. The designers took advantage of all occasions to underscore the foundation of their design vocabulary in squares as decorative elements, from the exaggerated right angles of oversized parquet floors, carpets, grid-covered wall panels, and custom lighting fixtures in the walls at every landing in the stair, to the logo at reception desks.

The eighty partner offices were each custom designed in unison with the established vocabulary of the rest of the space by members of a special design team over an eighteen-month period. Although lighting, carpet, and work-wall systems remained constant, the partners could have the seating, desk, and conference or lounge furniture of their choice.

The client considered their previous space to be too overtly institutional and over-lit, so the Gensler designers were asked to develop creative lighting solutions for the new multifaceted space. A system of indirect and broad color spectrum warm fluorescent tubes was employed rather than direct lighting in the secretarial and word processing areas. Indirect lighting solutions were used in the cafeteria, and all conference rooms have indirect lighting over the tables. A combination of fluorescent and incandescent lighting, utilizing a warmly rendered lamp, help maintain a non-institutional ambiance while maintaining energy code requirements.

The interconnecting stair links practice floors twenty through thirty and the reception areas are located on every other floor; support functions are situated on floors ten to thirteen. For the approximately 500,000-rentable-square-foot project the Gensler team also designed a major conference center, a 300-person full-service cafeteria, litigation center, and major computer facility.

Davis Polk & Wardwell is one of the most technically innovative law firms and sets the trends for others in the profession. The designers were challenged by their need to incorporate many of these innovations into the space.

Audiovisual, teleconferencing, and computer capabilities, were designed in the conferencing center, with high quality audio conferencing in all conference rooms. The client was extremely concerned about the need for a network of personal computers at every workstation as well as redundant fiberoptic technology within double risers. The risers were then wired from the main computer facility to a communications room on each floor, housing the required mechanical and electrical equipment. In order to facilitate maintenance and eventual changes, the designers located these rooms in the same location on each floor. A systematic wire management system on all floors permits relocation and change as required.

Every five years during the twenty-year lease, Davis Polk & Wardwell will have the option of acquiring two or three additional floors amounting to 190,000 additional square feet. The design for the space had to reflect these conditions. This complex and innovative project was brought in on schedule and under budget. Gensler also won the *American Bar Association Journal's* 1993 Law Office Design Competition for this project.

The location of the library on a "non-practice" floor allows the attorneys efficent access to contiguous stacks on a floorplate more suitable in size and layout.

Reflected indirect flourescent combined with direct incandescent lighting produces a warm yet energy-efficient working atmosphere.

An elegant cafeteria provides a quality environment for employees.

The floorplate maximized working efficiencies between attorneys, support staff, and other support functions.

Typical associate office which is a carpetable area of 10 feet x 15 feet to enable future double occupancy of all associate size offices.

Typical staff support workstations. Light covers and a warm fluorescent tube, rather than direct lighting, are used in secretarial and word processing areas.

HarperCollins Publishers is the consolidation of three companies: Harper San Francisco, which publishes religious and "new age" materials; Collins Publishers, which creates large-format illustrated books on art and photography; and The Understanding Business, a publisher of informational guides and manuals such as The Smart Yellow Pages. Gensler was approached by the newly consolidated company to act as an agent on all aspects of creating their new space, including selection of real estate, lease negotiations, telecommunications, and data consulting. Once the two-story, 55,236-square foot office space in San Francisco's Levi Plaza was selected, Gensler set out to create a design that would meet HarperCollins' various space requirements while creating interiors that are not overly corporate-looking. **The Gensler design had to reflect the individual character of the three distinct business entities and create a coherent atmosphere for the newly-combined 150 employee staff.** Because each unit was to retain a certain measure of autonomy, the project defined three separate parts, each with its own unique personality unified by design concepts that blend together both aesthetically and operationally.

As the three companies had never worked together before and knew little about each other, the immediate challenge was to enhance communication among them. The client also required an atmosphere that would be environmentally sound, and that would closely respect budget and schedule.

HarperCollins wanted a spirited office environment designed to withstand constant use and intended for a casual work style. People who visit the HarperCollins office are not teams of corporate clients who need to be impressed, but rather writers who usually arrive individually, tend to dress and work informally, and are in the same business as their publishers. (The work of this publishing house also clearly shared many characteristics with advertising agencies that Gensler had worked with previously.) **The designers set out to create an environment that would support the ways in which a highly creative staff works and interacts.** The design required the integration of five computer hardware systems, accomplished through a system that not only networks office hardware, but also links the office to systems around the world. The design had to accommodate rapidly evolving computer technology, multiple department libraries, and also foster easy communication among the three new divisions.

The designers created a prominent steel interconnecting stair as a central unifying element within the space. Intended as a gathering place, the stair is surrounded by reading areas and a library which lines a "Main Street," a focal corridor that unites all the various spaces. A library shared by Collins and The Understanding Business is located at the top of the staircase. It becomes clear in this space that there are distinct businesses operating under one roof. The Harper group is located on the first floor and part of the second, which it shares with Collins and The Understanding Business. The Collins space is

HarperCollins Publishers

Blond woods, shiny metals, and curvilinear detailing keep the space from feeling too corporate and serious.

Curves and visual details help soften and break up the large floor expanse.

a contemporary, relaxed environment with ambient lighting, soft green carpeting, and maple detailing. The Harper unit, which was planned as approximately fifty percent private offices and fifty percent open plan workstations, was designed as an informal non-corporate space which also makes extensive use of ambient lighting. The designers created a vocabulary for the space that incorporates traditional textures such as patterned carpeting, and industrial finishes such as wire mesh, formaldehyde-free exterior grade particle board, and cork floors that require minimal maintenance. For The Understanding Business, Gensler designers were asked to replicate certain elements that were dear to the company in its previous space. Industrial materials, including charcoal-colored floor coverings were coupled with steel detailing and glossy, hard wall coverings.

After careful consideration of the type of company that HarperCollins Publishers would become and the work they were involved with, Gensler created a design that was open and playful in its suggestion of picture books and storytelling. Immediately upon entering the space, visitors are greeted by a colorful mural by artist Anne Field representing the history of the company in large, exotic, richly colored images. On a pedestal to the left, the designers created a large white metal form that duplicates the open pages of a book and bears the company logo. In the conference room, solid cherry tables and heavy ash chairs were chosen because they would be durable enough to withstand the traffic of a constant flow of informal meetings.

Reading is a daily requirement for many Harper Collins employees and Gensler designed places specifically for that purpose. Several departmental libraries scattered throughout the facility are used to display the firm's products and vary in shape and size, from built-into-the wall shelves along the straight or curved walls of "Main Street," to a low bookcase in the reception area. The second floor lunchroom has a reading area with access to three balconies that provide pleasant outdoor space for reading. Throughout the space, small wall-mounted multi-level racks form a continuous piece of metal that serves as a display rack for current volumes.

The Gensler design met both budgetary and scheduling requirements for the client while still creating a distinctive environment for the three divisions to grow together. Significant savings were achieved through selective improvements and negotiating with manufactures, suppliers, and the landlord.

Looking from reception area into adjoining conference room used for formal meetings and informal employee gatherings. One-of-a-kind books on display are protected behind locked, wire mesh doors.

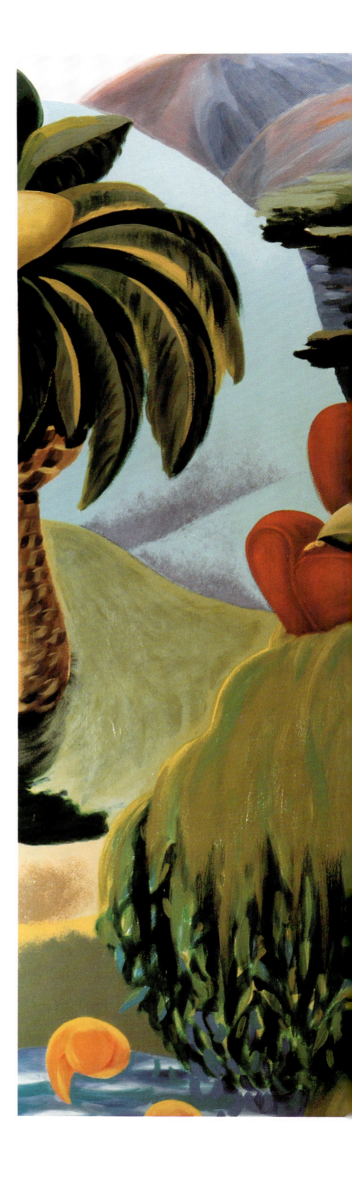

The reception and conference rooms are paired for large staff events by pivoted doors painted with an allegorical mural depicting the company's image.

Section of 80-foot-long library connects to the reception area.

Offices have glass doors to foster a sense of accessibility among employees who sit in modular workstations. Ambient lighting adds to the sense of casual ease.

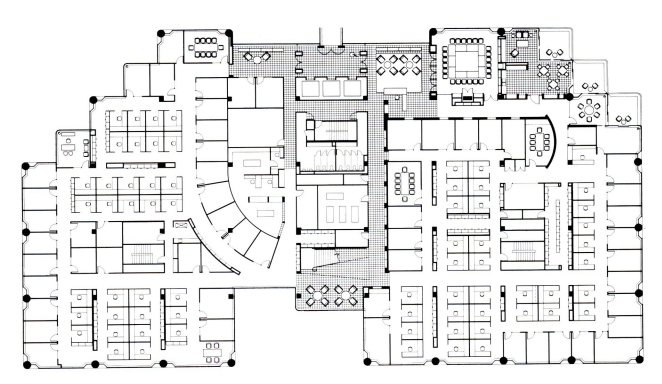

This office consolidates three disparate companies, yet allows each unit to retain a certain measure of autonomy.

In 1991, MCI Communications Corp. made the decision to relocate the world headquarters of its Information Technologies/Information Systems Division from the Washington, D.C. area to a sixty-one-acre site in Colorado Springs, Colorado. MCI was faced with the need to expand, contain costs, and improve the quality of the work environment for their employees. Gensler provided comprehensive master planning, architectural design, and interior planning and design services for this massive project.

The project included the renovation of two existing buildings on the site and the construction of six new buildings, all linked by a fifty-six-foot-high, skylight-studded atrium. Gensler began with a master plan for the campus before proceeding with the design for the additional buildings. There is a landscaped garden about the size of two football fields in the center of the eight-building, U-shaped complex. The garden not only creates a valuable space for employees, but also fosters a sense of community and stimulates creativity. In addition, the complex hosts a 125-seat auditorium, a customer service center, and an employee training facility. **MCI asked the Gensler architects, planners, and designers to create an environment that would "achieve creativity by serendipitous event."**

MCI was anxious to occupy the new Colorado Springs site as quickly as possible, and the Gensler team agreed to a demanding completion schedule that presented both the design and construction teams with unique challenges. The team remodeled 200,000 square feet in the former warehouse manufacturing areas of the two existing buildings to accommodate the initial 1,000 transferring employees, while the rest of the site remained under construction. By working closely with the MCI advisors and their contractor, Gensler was able to establish a plan to minimize the disruption of the company's work flow after occupation of the space.

The decision to incorporate a precast concrete structure allowed construction to begin during the severe Colorado winter. By closing off the structure with the curtain wall and roofing systems, the architects were able to dedicate valuable time to completing the interior construction while waiting for early spring weather to complete the exterior stone facades.

The design of the permanent facilities began in August of 1991, and by September 15, the developmental plan for the site had been approved by the MCI advisors. By March of 1992, Gensler completed renovation of 50,000 square feet of existing space and the first 135,000 square feet of office structure were in use by July. The first phase of the project was completed in October of 1993. In all, 1,000 existing employees, and an additional 2,500 new workers, were relocated into 775,000 square feet of space. The impending transfer of employees from MCI's Washington, D.C. office accelerated the schedule and required the highest levels of coordination and teamwork among Gensler, the general contractor, and the MCI management team. The project became an example of the best aspects of

MCI Communications Corp.

Page 134
Sunset overview of campus with mountains in background.

Page 135
Detail of rotunda feature on main entry of building.

Below
"The Reserve," a place where employees can eat, meet informally, or just relax and enjoy the spectacular views.

"partnering," and the result is one of Colorado's landmark corporate facilities.

The MCI facility borders on a residential neighborhood, and Gensler won support for the overall design of the campus from the neighboring community after numerous presentations in which the building and parking sites were described in detail. In order to protect the residents' views and maintain the natural beauty of the site, MCI purchased an additional sixty non-buildable acres adjacent to the site. The Gensler team situated the buildings to take advantage of the incredible views the location offered. To better integrate the buildings into the foothills, natural materials were employed, such as sandstone from the nearby Morrison formation, which was used extensively on the structures' exteriors. The site was also landscaped with indigenous plants.

Both the renovation and new construction were guided by MCI's desire to enhance employee productivity. Individual cubicles feature special fluorescent light fixtures made with unique aluminum coverings that significantly reduce glare. The MCI project was the first place in the world where this innovative lighting system was used. A spacious, open feeling was created by incorporating skylights and maintaining open access to expansive perimeter windows. Walkways are illuminated with recessed lighting to create an intimate, non-institutional atmosphere, and the same design vocabulary is used for the resource library areas and conference rooms.

The entire facility includes only six closed, private offices, four of which were intended for visitors. The designers incorporated a number of "war rooms," meeting areas, and team rooms into the overall design of the space in order to provide some private work areas. All the other workspaces and open plan areas were designed to facilitate MCI's high annual change and growth rate in a dynamic business arena. **The workstations and cubicles were designed into the space in such a way that workers could be moved within the space only by changing the individual's electronic mailbox number.**

Gensler worked with ITEL, MCI's internal telecommunications group, to determine the design and technological requirements of a 3,000-square-foot main distribution facility which features a raised computer floor, racks containing CPU's, and drivers needed for switching incoming as well as in-house calls. This switching center also serves three other MCI facilities.

East facade showing main entry to the campus.

The connectors between buildings offer access and views to The Reserve, as well as seating areas for casual employee interaction.

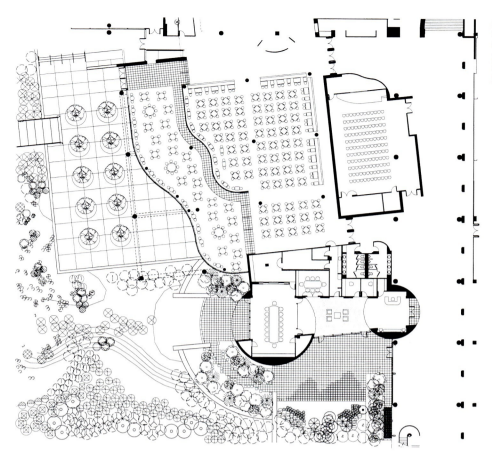

A 600-seat dining facility, show in plan, sits adjacent to state of-the-art training rooms, a high-tech Executive Briefing Center, and outdoor patios.

Cafeteria, with Servery in background, offers spectacular montain views. Employees can choose to dine indoors or on adjoining outdoor patios.

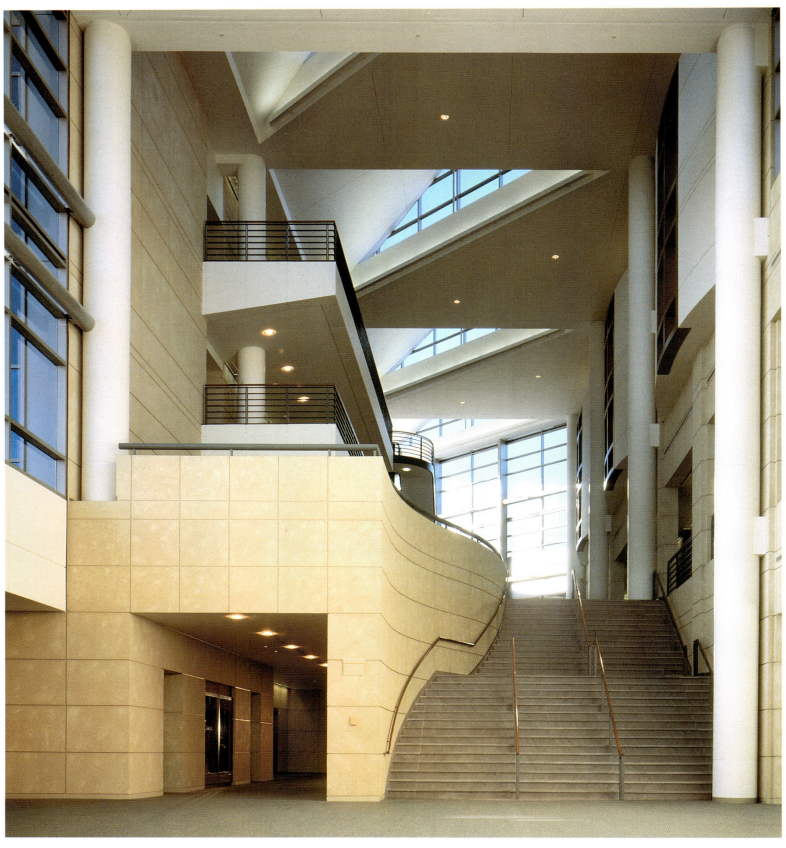

Previous pages
Stairs connect to the spine which serves as an open space for employee interaction, and a hall for changing exhibits of art and technology. The major common elements of the campus also open off this space.

Dramatic grand stair draws visitors from entry into the heart of the facility. En route, glass-fronted hall offers views to the Garden of the Gods.

Executive Briefing Center is used for private meetings and customer presentations. It offers client work rooms and a private patio.

Prefunction area for conference and training center.

View of open workstations. MCI's commitment to the open work environment is exemplified by the fact that in the entire 3,500 person campus there are only six private offices.

Staff Library combines research areas and quiet spaces for focused thinking.

State-of-the-art training facility is flexible for configuration into various presentation and teaching modes.

Morrison & Foerster, founded in San Francisco in 1883, is one of the leading law firms in the United States. The firm provides a full range of services both domestically and internationally and employs some 600 lawyers in various branch offices in cities such as New York, London, and Tokyo. The Palo Alto, California office represents clients from the various business sectors in the region, including semiconductors, computer hardware and software, telecommunications, and biotechnology. As a result, the sixty-one attorneys working in the office had specialized largely in corporate finance and litigation. When the firm acquired a practice in patents and intellectual properties, they were immediately confronted with new and different paper handling and storage needs. They turned to Gensler for help in establishing new design solutions for their rapidly evolving and expanding Palo Alto workplace.

Gensler created a master plan for Morrison & Foerster that was directed at solving the immediate space problems as well as planning for the firm's future needs. The attorneys did not want to move to a new location, so Gensler worked within the existing campus and consolidated the firm's activities from three buildings to two. During the replanning of the space, the designers took the opportunity to relocate the entry to a place at the center of the complex where it was more apparent to Morrison & Foerster's clients. The new, more centrally located lobby and conference center were built around a two-story space, the only relief from the low-slung buildings. **The design concept for this 65,000-square-foot branch office created an environment that promotes and reinforces innovative thinking, and presents a non-traditional image for the firm.**

While this branch of Morrison & Foerster wished to maintain a small-firm style, it is still part of the larger firm and taps its worldwide resources. Gensler had to respond to this very particular context: create a facility for a firm capable of providing intimate, personal contacts while functioning simultaneously on a global front. **The designers set out to create a law office for the 1990s, free from preconceptions of what law firms should look like, built for active use and ready for future evolution.** The Gensler plan for the space is a rethinking of the problems facing contemporary law firms, and lays the foundation for the innovative flexibility the firm required. While the project was still in the planning phase, it became clear that, in addition to an efficient use of the space, ergonomics, and attorney privacy, the staff members' main concern was having sufficient light in their workplaces. The designers, although working within a limited budget, incorporated clerestory glass and up-lit ceilings throughout to create a remarkable sense of spaciousness all through the facility. There were also many columns within the space that the previous design tried to hide or rationalize. The designers integrated the columns into the support workstations, eliminating the building's dictated divisions.

The most important concern for Gensler was how the newly-acquired patent group would be integrated

Morrison & Foerster

The entire facility was conceived as a series of overlapping planes centered on a jog in the building.

Facing page
The relocated lobby and conference center is organized around a two-story central hearth.

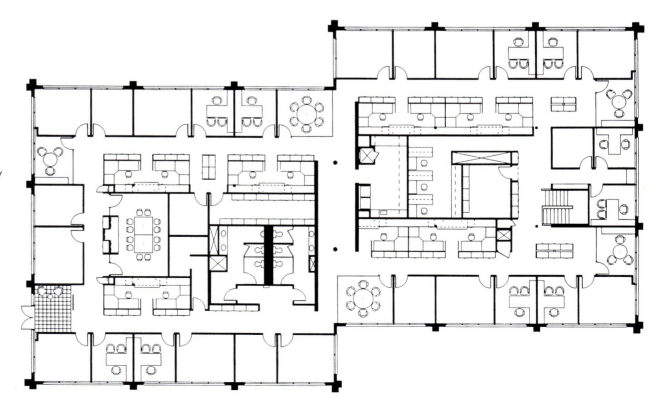

into the various office systems. There were immediate practical concerns: patent attorneys work with a different size of files than litigation lawyers, and the file storage units that Morrison & Foerster maintained previously could not accommodate this different-sized paper, let alone its overwhelming volume. In their traditional litigation practice, the Morrison & Foerster lawyers maintained standard forms which were generated and kept within their computers, a system that allowed them to fax and file with the courts electronically. Typical of many law firms, Morrison & Foerster's need for paper, and paper storage, was diminishing as more computers with larger screens for imaging documents, and a more computer-literate professional staff entered the firm. While their litigation practice could operate smoothly electronically, the patent practice existed and flourished on quite a different level. Many of the patents Morrison & Foerster dealt with were established in the last century and all of the documentation surrounding the patent practice, except for the most recently generated documents, were on paper. **In order to keep the potentially overwhelming clutter under control, the office plan had to address the management of all paper sizes and the various work styles that generate the documents.** The need for flexibility in volume and size of files for both the attorneys and secretaries was primarily addressed through the use of a standardized file system that was flexible enough to address both patent and non-patent attorney needs.

In addition to the integration of the patent attorneys, Morrison & Foerster explained to the designers that the nature of their business was changing. They were retaining fewer junior associates as clients began to require more partner involvement. At the same time, because of increased computer literacy, the partners were more involved in the production of their own documents. In response to the changing ratio of partners to support staff, the designers arranged attorneys, assistants, and secretaries in flexible work teams or "neighborhoods." The designers then established areas dubbed "mini-marts" housing decentralized fax machines, copiers, printers, supplies, and coffee for groups of two of the adjacent "neighborhood" work zones. By locating many of the support services nearby, these "mini-marts," which are used heavily after regular business hours, make it unnecessary for secretaries to walk long distances from their desks to access services. These centralized areas also allow for obsolete equipment to be easily replaced as technology changes. In addition to the mini-mart, the designers provided every neighborhood with a shared "working" conference room. These small conference rooms afford full views, with windows that allow as much natural light as possible, and were specifically designed to respond to the firm's increasing number of internal meetings. Providing each "neighborhood" with its own conference room helped establish a sense of community among the employees, and a strong sense of belonging to the space. The rooms are equipped with full-height markerboards, complex audiovisual equipment, "wired" team-oriented, flexibly designed tables and ergonomic chairs. One of the conference rooms was also designed to accommodate video conference capabilities.

The amount of change anticipated at the Morrison & Foerster Palo Alto facility required a great deal of flexibility in the furniture systems. A slat wall behind the secretarial stations allows for frequent reconfiguration of a variety of standard organizing trays which are easily movable and eliminate clutter at the desktop. There are also spaces for files that accommodate either the standard legal files or the patent files. Although this area appears custom-made, each of the elements is composed of standard, inexpensive products. Gensler employed a similar strategy in the attorney offices. Working within a standard furniture budget, the designers created a work wall which doubles the usable surface.
The Gensler designers won the *American Bar Association Journal* 1995 Small Law Firm Design Award for this project.

Central corridor showing working conference room at end, checkered wall housing "mini-mart," and secretarial station.

Secretarial stations are freestanding height-adjustable furniture enclosed by flexibly-sized standard files.

Within the private office, a work wall doubles as a usable surface by providing a flexible paper stacking and organizing area.

Ambient-lit secretarial stations with ergonomic furniture and slat wall on right.

MasterCard International hired Gensler to work with a consulting engineer to evaluate buildings in Manhattan, Westchester, and Connecticut for the relocation of the firm's world headquarters. The team finally selected an I.M. Pei-designed building, which is set in a beautiful fifty-acre suburban corporate park in rural Purchase, New York. Constructed in 1984, it had been initially occupied by Nestle and IBM. MasterCard preferred the building because it had a number of advantages over a Manhattan high-rise. The facility clearly met three company objectives: it was convenient to Manhattan and metropolitan New York airports, its cost was much lower than the Manhattan locations under consideration, and above all, the facility was convenient to MasterCard's work force. In addition to satisfying the company's stated objectives, the facility promised savings of $250 million over the following fifteen years. Moreover, in addition to its clean, abstract lines, fine materials, and verdant setting, the 432,000-square-foot building offered the advantage of large floor areas on each level and a simple, horizontal organization. The concrete waffle-slab floor structure and thirty-by-thirty-foot column grid offered the flexibility to create new, open office arrangements that would allow MasterCard to deliver its services efficiently.

The vice president of MasterCard's administrative services, in charge of the relocation, admired the "museum quality" of Pei's classic glass, concrete, and travertine building, but quickly communicated to the Gensler team his concern about how his company's employees would get to work, and how they would interact with each other once on the job. Gensler understood the need to put the employees first, and designed the entire workplace around their needs. The challenge of working with a building by a renowned architect was overshadowed by that of making certain that every individual had a well-lit, comfortable, and well-connected work space. Margo Grant Walsh, managing principal of Gensler's New York office and design principal of the eleven-person Gensler team working on the MasterCard project, explained that "even though MasterCard was moving into an existing building, there was still much work to be done to ensure that the new worldwide headquarters accurately reflected the organization's unique corporate culture."

Gensler's challenge was to design a facility for the evolving operations of this world-class organization while respecting the integrity of the architecturally significant structure. The base building is composed of two three-story pavilions linked at the center by a third pavilion. This third connecting pavilion serves as both a lobby and administration service block. The Gensler designers retained Pei's monumental staircase in the central pavilion and the ramps (or roundabouts) in the office pavilions. This left the building's simple, clear circulation pattern intact for easy connection among floors, allowing for ready interaction among business groups and individuals working in teams. The designers simply restored the existing architecture by conserving and repairing finishes, updating lighting, and providing furnishings to

MasterCard International

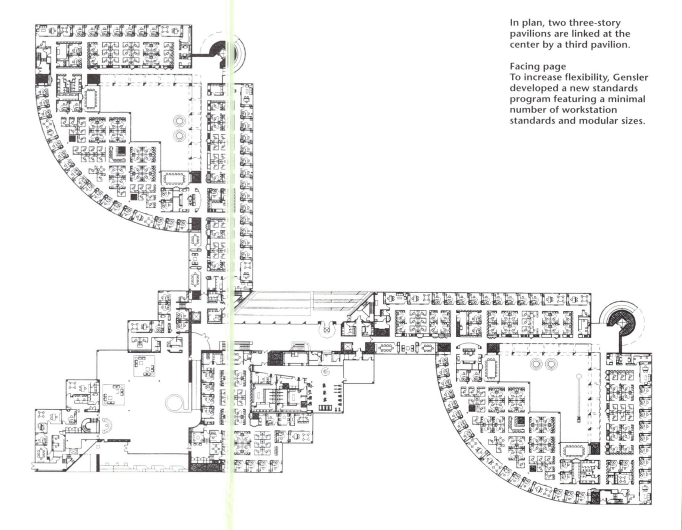

In plan, two three-story pavilions are linked at the center by a third pavilion.

Facing page
To increase flexibility, Gensler developed a new standards program featuring a minimal number of workstation standards and modular sizes.

Previous spread
Staircases and open areas were retained to foster interaction among business groups and staff.

Private office seen through curved glass wall. Selected manufacturers of private office furniture competed in the bidding process.

Employees are provided comfortable relaxation areas, such as fitness center, locker room, and cafeteria.

enhance the design of the base building.

A few larger alterations were required to bring the 1984 building up to current standards. One of the major changes included rewiring the building for new telecommunications, computer technologies, and digitally controlled lighting. The designers also installed new electrical and HVAC systems chosen to save energy and lower operational costs. MasterCard required fitness and day-care centers for their employees and the Gensler designers worked with outside consultants to design these new on-site facilities. In addition, significant enhancements to the parking garage at the rear of the site were made and large visitors' offices added in the central pavilion, as well as training areas and meetings rooms.

MasterCard's main criteria for the design were flexibility and synergy. In response to these needs, the Gensler team created flexible, open environments. For the interiors of the office pavilions, Gensler established a design vocabulary based on low partitions, even lighting, and exclusive use of glass and aluminum for the walls to separate the middle managers' offices located at the perimeter of the building from the workstations located around the open atriums. (This arrangement is precisely the opposite of that adopted by IBM when it occupied the space.) The Gensler design allows natural light to be shared by all employees. **To maximize flexibility and increase employee interaction, a new program was developed, featuring a minimal number of workstation standards and modular sizes, as well as a universal plan with uniform distribution of office and workstation types, conference, and support areas.** Senior vice president office sizes were established at twelve feet by twelve feet; executive vice president offices at twelve feet by twenty-four feet. Like many of the decisions the designers made, the choice to retain the interior staircases was driven by a need to foster interaction among business groups and staff. The same concept encouraged the designers to use glass office fronts and forty-eight-inch workstation panel heights—design elements that encourage communication and create views.

During the planning and design phase, the Gensler team presented MasterCard with foamcore mock-ups of workstations and office layouts. The designers then selected manufacturers of private office furniture, systems, conference furniture, seating, and files to participate in a competitive bid for the various jobs. The designers used a P-shaped desk top capable of accommodating small meetings of up to five people for the large visitors' offices. The Gensler team's modest approach to the renovation of public areas resulted in a significant budget reduction for the project.

Throughout the facility, work groups are arranged in flexible, open office layouts connected by E-mail networks. The company is able to adapt quickly and efficiently to new personnel situations by simply moving partitions. Although all the office spaces were rebuilt, replacing the existing maze-like configuration with a universal plan of open workstations and perimeter offices, Gensler's initial activities focused on providing plans that were universal and modular in concept to meet the ever-changing needs of the MasterCard organization. Gensler was successful by limiting workplace standards and increased flexibility.

The Gensler designers' goal was to accurately reflect the MasterCard personality throughout every aspect of the building while staying within the cost objectives and convenience of the client. The new MasterCard International headquarters looks as though it was built expressly for them, not like a building that has been reengineered. It represents the thoughtful transformation of an architectural icon into a new, functional environment.

Private offices are furnished with P-shaped desk top to accommodate small meetings.

Work groups are arranged in flexible, open office layouts to encourage flexibility and synergy.

In order to save a necessary $6 million per year in operating costs, Chevron sold its historic headquarters building in San Francisco, California. The building, located at 225 Bush Street, had housed Chevron's executive offices for seventy-five years. The proceeds from the sale were invested in the renovation of two nearby company-owned buildings, adjacent to each other at 575 and 555 Market Street.

Gensler was retained by Chevron, a giant of the petroleum industry, to renovate and upgrade the existing buildings into one cohesive world headquarters facility. Chevron's chairman, Ken Derr, wanted the renovation and relocation project, which went into construction in March of 1994, to reflect the company's accomplishments, become an asset to the local community, and make a positive statement to employees, stockholders, and customers.

In addition to the adaptation of some of the spaces for new uses, the Gensler team reorganized the building's orientation to both Market Street and what was an undistinguished garden between the two buildings. In the new design, the entrance to the 575 Market Street building was shifted away from the street to open towards the 555 entry and toward the expanded garden and new landscaping. Working with the landscape designers at Hellmuth, Obata & Kassabaum, Gensler created a garden that became the point of entry for both buildings and a communicating pedestrian link between them. The landscaped network of walkways and a central plaza spanning the garden have since become a much-loved public viewing space enjoyed by many of the city's residents and visitors. Two matching bronze entrance doors were designed to unite the buildings and create a visual vocabulary between them that is then continued in the interior. **Chevron wanted a corporate "home" that simultaneously defined and expressed Chevron's character and corporate culture. The designers concentrated on creating an open, bright atmosphere throughout the facility that, wherever possible, would foster eye contact and communication among employees and visitors.**

The Gensler team designed the new entries and lobbies to underscore a notion of Chevron's place within the history of American industry and project an idea of the responsibility that Chevron has taken on as a major international petroleum company. A dark bronze cylinder is installed in the lobby, which contains the revolving entrance door. This cylindrical form is repeated in the design of the two circular display cases in the lobby. Eight feet in diameter, these impressive cases were created to display rotating exhibitions of Chevron's international collection of artifacts as well as exhibitions documenting the company's history. For the security station, also located in the lobby, the vocabulary of bronze motifs is continued.

Millwork is used extensively throughout the project, much of it faced with eucalyptus veneer, in addition to walnut, cherry, and anigre woods. Before accepting the use of such woods, Chevron insisted that the designers provide certification of the sources. Even the anigre, which is often improperly harvested,

Chevron Corporation

At the end of the entrance lobby at 575 Market Street is a circular bronze showcase displaying Chevron memorabilia.

Elevator lobby with new elevator cabs and upgraded finishes.

40th floor plan. Executive floor with chairman's office and executive staff.

The 40th floor waiting area with display cabinet showcasing the corporation's collection of artifacts, gathered from the 93 countries where Chevron works.

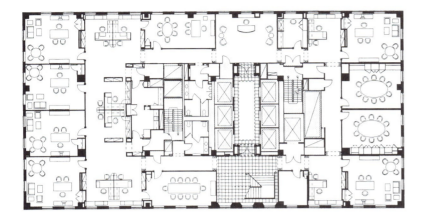

arrived from a sustainable source. The Gensler designers extended Chevron's insistence on this matter into part of the design vocabulary for the project, demonstrating Chevron's commitment to the environment worldwide, extending beyond the comfort of their San Francisco headquarters. **The project design expresses this sense of global, environmental responsibility.**

In the 555 Market Street tower, the Gensler designers transformed an underutilized second-floor cafeteria space into a column-free conference center, made available to all employees. A movable wall was incorporated to allow the space to assume various configurations depending on ever-changing space requirements. Like the new boardroom, this facility hosts state-of-the-art audiovisual equipment. Screens were designed to disappear behind sliding doors and the room was conceived in such a way as to permit a television station to hook up and broadcast directly from the space.

The Gensler team's design vocabulary is based on consistency of materials throughout the facility to unify the entire space and make these two separate towers into a cohesive headquarters facility.

For the support staff workstations, a union of a freestanding, marble-topped, cherry wood credenza with both file and simple storage space are used together with a somewhat more traditional secretarial station in the same cherry wood. The complete workstation is equipped with indirect lighting and smart technology.

The boardroom is a perfect matrimony between state-of-the-art information technology and traditional, understated elegance. From the boardroom table, an LED device controls all of the audiovisual and lighting systems in the room by a touch screen. By choosing "slide presentation," for example, the window shades go down automatically, the lights dim, and the doors slide open to reveal the rear projection screen. Other options on the touch screen system include cable television, VCR, laser disc, audio cassette, document projection, and large-format computer screen viability. The information technology serving these spaces is visually subdued, intentionally overshadowed by design elements that nod to the traditional space without ever being busy, cluttered, fussy, or overly detailed.

While the buildings are fully equipped with the

Executive secretarial station has a comfortable chair and pull-out writing surface for visitors' use while waiting.

latest smart technology, it is largely invisible to visitors. The executive floors are equipped for audiovisual teleconferencing, and a small nearby crisis center is also equipped with hook ups for additional telephones and computers. The design called for a boardroom that would allow individuals to call up a large variety of lighting and projection options, and the large conference center was designed with microphones in the ceiling, as well as facilities for slides, computers, laser discs, etc. This advanced technology goes beyond the interior of the building; a port on the street provides hook-up for mobile units from television stations.

This project involved a very standard design process, from programming to construction administration; however, Chevron's corporate culture is based on the idea of a consensus decision-making process. Therefore, the Gensler team had to filter all planning and design decisions through what is known as the "Chevron Project Development and Execution Process," the company's standardized procedure for decision-making. This procedure simply mandates five phases with a representative from each process that will be involved in any project. Suggestions and cost estimates could be made early on and alternative ideas reviewed before final decisions were made. **The Gensler team was never asked to redesign since they were participants in the management thought process at the initial stage of the project. The success of their design lies in a building that simultaneously speaks of corporate power, responsibility, and respect for its employees.**

On the 40th floor stairway, an enticing view to the surrounding Bay Area.

Conference center dining and seminar area. The conference center was converted from a former cafeteria.

Private dining room and lounge area on the 38th floor.

555 Market Street conference center with phone vestibules and dining area.

Hoffmann-La Roche is one of the world's leading research-based health-care groups, active in the discovery, development, manufacture, and marketing of pharmaceuticals and diagnostic systems. For over half a century, Building One, a handsome, Art Deco facility at the company's national headquarters in Nutley, New Jersey, had become an emblem of their prominence in the industry. However, by the early 1990s, the much-loved building's infrastructure could no longer accommodate the latest information technology, and its traditional compartmentalized layout was not encouraging the sort of teamwork Hoffmann-La Roche was seeking, aimed at reducing by half their time-to-market for new pharmaceuticals.

Hoffmann-La Roche held a competition to select the designers for the seven-story, 225,000-square-foot base building and its interiors, to replace Building One. The team of The Hillier Group and Gensler won the competition. Gensler then executed a number of Hoffmann-La Roche-identified business objectives for the new facility. Gensler understood that in today's fiercely competitive pharmaceutical industry, Hoffmann-La Roche employees would need to be able to work closely in cross-functional teams to move important new drugs through development, the FDA, and to the market as quickly as possible. **The Gensler designers had to create an environment where marketing people, sales people, and doctors engaged in clinical trials could all work in teams.** In order to meet these requirements, the Gensler designers completely dispelled the notion of hierarchies in office space and adopted a one-size-fits-all "universal" office plan. All employees were organized in the new Building One, from vice presidents to secretaries, in the same seventy-square-foot workstations clustered into "neighborhood" group work areas. **The Gensler team designed every aspect of the new floor plan to enhance teamwork, communications, and organizational flexibility.**

The plan encourages group interaction and informal, impromptu meetings while also offering individually controlled, private workspaces for each of the 850 employees. Meeting areas, studios, studies, coffee bars, and hallways were all planned to potentially encourage the interaction and productivity that Hoffmann-La Roche desired. An eighty-person capacity conference facility is located on the ground floor; other floors host meeting areas ranging in capacity from four to twelve people. In addition, each floor hosts two 800 square-foot "studios." These large, very flexible rooms divide each floor of the compact building into four smaller quadrants and provide a visual connection to the exterior through two-story bay windows. These "studios" make use of natural light and provide a sense of open space ideal for the sort of flexible teaming functions they were designed to host.

A principal component of the Building One work environment was the creation of individual "studies." The Gensler designers took an old idea, the scholar's Kabinet, and transformed it into a high performance workplace. **These spaces are intended to provide a personal "think cell," to which staff**

Hoffmann-La Roche, Inc.

The design of Building One will encourage unscheduled encounters. The plan locates support spaces, such as restrooms, elevators and convenience areas, in a centralized position to put them closer to people.

Building One was designed so that the average distance from the study (workstation) to a meeting area will be 50 feet, but never more than 90 feet. The perimeter is left open for common use, with more public spaces in the middle.

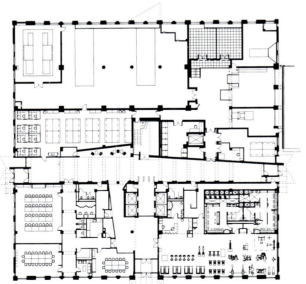

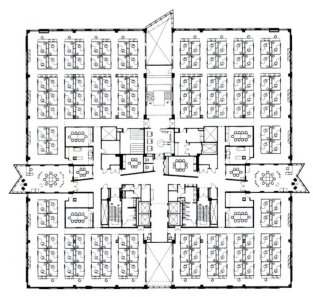

Seating area adjacent to display. Staff encounter a variety of spaces in which to work, and a consistent layout from floor to floor provides better orientation and circulation.

Conference room takes advantage of building architecture. Building One has more meeting areas than the rest of the buildings at the Nutley site combined.

members may retire to work individually, hold private conversations, and access their technology while also remaining open to more public communications. Each "study," a design which Gensler has patented, is wired by cables that drop from the ceiling into columns that feed electricity and technology to the workplace. The glass construction of the "study" provides staff with the advantage of an "open-door" working style, while simple sliding doors may be closed and locked to offer the quiet and individual focus of a private office. Each "study" is also equipped with its own Personal Environment Module (PEM) of environmental controls which provide the occupant with the ability to control air, radiant heating, light levels, and even masking noise.

The incorporation of the "study" in Hoffmann-La Roche's Building One is an example of Gensler's ability to use furniture as architecture. The designers developed certain generic performance requirements for the studies and called on three manufacturers to interpret the specifications with their own components. Working from Gensler's full-size mock-up, the Italian office furniture company Unifor was able to meet the requirements and move into production. The resulting "studies" are quality spaces in which every detail has been very carefully considered as a specific piece of industrial design.

A consistent floor-to-floor layout fosters simpler orientation and circulation for staff and visitors. The Gensler plan locates support spaces, such as rest rooms, elevators, and convenience areas, in a centralized position to put them closer to people. The designers left the perimeter open for common use, placing additional public spaces in the center of the plan. While the studies were designed as universal elements, their placement is anything but regular. Some are located near exterior walls, others are closer to the core. Some group spaces host more of these individually-sized workplaces, while others were designated as more intimate working "neighborhoods."

Building One is designed to be a major part of the information superhighway at Hoffmann-La Roche. Throughout the space, some seventy hoteling stations can be found—places with telephones and computer connections for use by visiting employees from both the United States and abroad, temporary staff, drug development and marketing teams, including contractors and consultants. Staff members are also provided with analog and digital connections, and with direct attachment to fiberoptic cables, which provide fax communication capabilities from each computer as well as teleconferencing in each "study." At the end of each workstation cluster, the Gensler team located power "chimneys" which rise to the ceiling to meet all power and data. **This simple distribution of power resulted in tremendous savings, since power distribution did not have to run through the floor, and all work could be done within the individual workspaces.** In addition to incorporating the latest technology, dangerous materials were also avoided, and a special HEPA air filtration system was installed to keep the building's air as clean as possible.

Perhaps the most distinctive feature of Building One is the light, airy quality of the overall work environment. **The glass-walled facility is the first in this part of the world to use a specially made glass with horizontal prisms that bend natural light up to a highly reflective, sound-absorbing ceiling.** As a result, outside light is drawn forty percent deeper into the center of each floor. Special fixtures are also incorporated into the tops of the workwalls to provide additional indirect ambient light when the natural light is not sufficient.

The density of the Hoffmann-La Roche project might lead observers to the initial conclusion that the designers set out to create a space optimization plan, rather than a design grounded in the necessity to create a high-performance workplace placing its occupants first. But the latter is the case. Gensler's design for the new Building One will provide the Hoffmann-La Roche staff with the tools they will need to meet their business objectives.

Typical study area for small meetings. Spontaneous interaction among staff is encouraged.

View of typical core area with group work space.

One of three typical coffee bars, located near the stairways for easy access by staff.

Looking into interior of a "study." These personal workspaces are arranged in "neighborhoods" for improved interaction among team members.

Close-up of Personal Environmental Module System. While seen as an extremely private space, the study is also conducive to interaction. Three people can meet comfortably in each "study."

Gensler was retained to restore and refurbish the Board of Governors of the Federal Reserve System boardroom. For this complex project, the Gensler team designed lighting, acoustic systems, fabrics, rugs, and furniture, and installed a state-of-the-art technology system.

The Federal Reserve Boardroom is housed in a 1936 building on Constitution Avenue in Washington, D.C. It had not undergone any repair or refurbishment in nearly twenty years when Gensler was asked to take on the project. The furnishings in this important workplace were in great disrepair. An historically significant, hand-painted fresco map illustrating the location of each of the original Federal Reserve banks in the United States was soiled by pollutants, and the technology that served the space was hopelessly inadequate.

An earlier plan to modernize the space had been abandoned, and this time the Federal Reserve Chairman specifically requested that the new design be consistent with the style of the original. **The designers were required not only to construct, renovate, and refurbish the space while working around the Federal Reserve Board's schedule, but were also given a mandate to create a state-of-the-art workplace without fundamentally changing the original structure.** Gensler was asked to retain the very highest regard for the historic nature of this meeting place while creating a new design and installing updated technology that would be camouflaged within the style of the original space. Images of the Boardroom are projected continuously around the world via television broadcasts, and this global dispersion of the image of the Federal Reserve has become an integral part of what the space represents and how it functions. While the style and proportions of the room clearly reflected the serious sensibility of the Federal design that prevailed in 1936, the daily technological demands placed upon the space by the Board and their staff, not to mention television crews and reporters, had seriously compromised the utility of the space. For example, before the renovation, presentations were still being made on wooden easels.

The centerpiece in the room is the new Gensler-designed board table. This table, a masterpiece of craftsmanship and technology, was designed so that from each of the twenty-six positions available around it, participants could make direct eye contact with anyone at any of the other positions along the table. The designers located twenty-six minute microphones around the perimeter of the table that were programmed to pick up normal conversational speech at each place and amplify the sound enough to be heard by everyone present. Federal law requires that all official meetings held in the room be recorded, so the designers integrated a recording system into the table which also hosts electrical and computer outlets. A "touch" panel screen is located within a drawer beneath the surface of the table at the Chairman's place. The screen allows for the manipulation of eight pre-set lighting schemes, along with electrical controls for the automated systems in

Board of Governors of the Federal Reserve System

While not a typical workplace, the Boardroom is nevertheless the scene of intensive collaboration and discussion used by many staff members in addition to the governors.

Close-up view of Boardroom, which underwent a subtle renovation to upgrade materials and incorporate state-of-the-art audiovisual technology.

the room. One touch to the screen lowers projection screens, closes window shades, and dims the lights within twenty seconds. Two retractable video projectors above the center of the table and electric projection screens at each end of the 100-foot long room provide everyone in the room with clear sightlines.

The technology incorporated into the room might seem excessive, but only because it is so unexpected in a space of this character. Everything about the decoration and order of the room seems completely at home within the building's historic character. The Gensler designers researched the original color palette used in the room and chose warm gray, pale gray, and soft gold as a point of departure for their new designs for the wool rug, silk drapery fabrics, and upholstered walls. Even ergonomically correct chairs were designed to resemble the 1936 originals.

Gensler's design for The Federal Reserve Boardroom highlights the importance of "invisible" intervention. **The designers were clearly challenged by the need to create an atmosphere that would underscore the historic importance of this workplace while simultaneously updating the facility to accommodate the technology necessary to tie the space to an ever-expanding global audience.**

Careful attention was given to preserving the historic character of the Boardroom.

Detail of carpet, custom made to enhance the original design.

The public has an opportunity to attend selected meetings in the Boardroom, so a sense of propriety and tradition was reinforced through furnishings.

Detail showing computer touch panel screen and other essential technology and audiovisual equipment easily accessible to the Chairman of the Federal Reserve Board.

Columbia/HCA, one of the largest health care service providers in the United States, hired ERS, a Los Angeles based call center management consulting firm, to a long-term contractual commitment to provide turn-key services for all of Columbia's customer service/call center projects throughout the U.S. With a keen understanding of the health care industry, ERS was charged with procuring the design, construction, and infrastructure teams as well as staffing and managing the operation of the first center built for Columbia/HCA in Bedford, Texas. Columbia/HCA needed a facility to handle the anticipated influx of telephone inquiries into their hospital and physician programs and referrals resulting from a new national "branding" campaign. ERS was responsible for retaining the entire team, including the architect, general contractor, and vendors for furniture, security, hardware, etc. They also hired key staff members, customized and implemented required software programs, and actually led the daily administrative and operational activities of the center.

ERS, rather than Columbia/HCA, handled the selection of Gensler as the design firm for the project. ERS relied heavily upon the Gensler team of planners, architects, and designers for opinions and recommendations that would make the 46,000-square-foot, abandoned WalMart retail facility into an environment marked by quality and team spirit. The goals formulated jointly by Gensler and ERS were aimed toward ensuring a successful project within a very aggressive completion schedule. The team was successful; Gensler began architectural work for the call center in January of 1996, and construction was completed just six months later.

Columbia/HCA required that the renovation include an open area to house 313 agent workstations. In order to meet this need the Gensler team established an open office plan that occupies the majority of the interior space. In addition to administrative offices, Columbia/HCA also required training and conference facilities. **Columbia/HCA envisioned their new center as one that could handle an undetermined increase in the number of incoming calls as new marketing and branding campaigns were created. Keeping this in mind, Gensler designed the space with the capability to provide solutions with built-in flexibility for easy expansion and change.**

The design required an open environment that would support the management philosophy of "empowered teaming" while de-emphasizing the inhumane size of the large floorplate. The designers organized the functional elements of the call center to maximize employee time and avoid unnecessary movement, bearing in mind employee satisfaction with the hopes of keeping turnover low. A "circulation boulevard" was created to connect the main entry to the open offices and other staff areas beyond. Since each workstation is used by various employees on a constantly changing schedule of shifts, the design needed to provide each staff member with a space for personal items that was distinct from the workstations. Multi-colored lockers were installed for this purpose within the "circulation boulevard."

Columbia/HCA Call Center

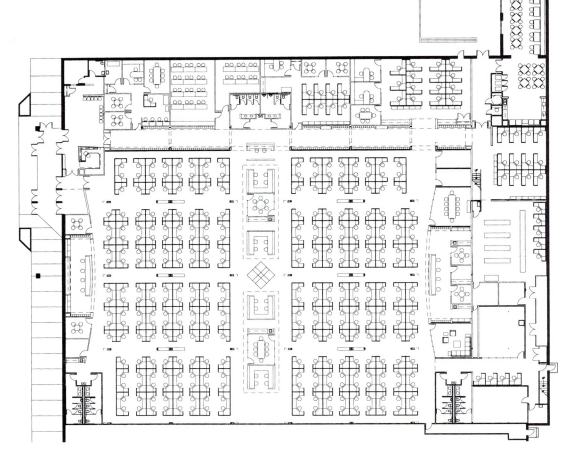

Gensler transformed a former store into an efficient and functional call center.

Administration area with private offices and break out space. Since most work is done in an open area, privacy and quiet time become essential to employees.

Reception Area showing perforated metal ceiling device used to break up the 14-foot-high ceilings.

Agent meeting rooms are provided for relaxation, small conferences, etc.

Open workstations arranged in clusters with a supervisor at the hub. Employees share seats, keeping private possessions in a locker.

The employee break room is located in what was formerly the Wall-Mart loading dock. The loading dock doors were filled with glass block to capture natural light.

Netscape Communications Corporation has quickly become the premier provider of software enabling users to exchange information and conduct commerce over the Internet and other global networks. Netscape is a young company with an innovative, pioneering spirit, offering a full line of client-server software to deliver secure communications, advanced performance, and point-and-click simplicity. Netscape is strongly committed to e-mail, collaborative software, and internal communication software.

On its Internet site, Netscape describes itself as "a cool place to work," and the Gensler team of designers and planners knew that this work environment must reflect the corporate culture to attract and retain the employees Netscape wanted.

Netscape Communications approached Gensler in July of 1996 with their need to quickly and inexpensively establish a high-performance, on-line workplace for its rapidly growing, youthful, and diverse workforce. By February of 1997, Gensler had designed and executed five buildings for Netscape with a total of 260,000 square feet of "wired" work space. By the end of 1997, the Gensler team completed the design and construction of an additional 339,000 square feet distributed across five buildings. Each of these buildings, on both the Mountain View and Sunnyvale, California campuses, presented unique opportunities for the Gensler planners, designers, and architects.

The first Gensler project for Netscape, Building 9, was slated to be completed on an extremely tight schedule in order to meet the corporation's critical need for technologically invested space. In late July, the Gensler team began designing the building interiors that would house the Netscape group responsible for developing and writing codes that secure Federal Internet communications. By September of the same year employees were already at work in the facility. This project, which incorporates a vinyl-tiled fish pond, free-standing message boards, and a flexible break-out area/conference suite, was designed and documented in approximately six weeks and constructed in about nine weeks.

Midway through the design phase, Netscape changed the program for Building 15 from administrative offices to the software engineering laboratories for a mail server-products development group. Building 14 (adjacent to Building 15) was designed specifically to contain state-of-the-art lab space for the development and testing of new Internet products. The design for these spaces blends informal conference areas and lounge spaces with an open office plan designed to minimize acoustical and visual disturbance. The core of Building 15 is compact while the support areas for Building 14 are clustered into service centers at the building's opposite ends. The inexpensive, flexible design vocabulary is based on the simple manipulation of sheetrock, tile ceiling elements, and bold graphics for both the walls and floors. The design concept is deceptively simple: all space is workspace, lounges offer data ports, electrical service, and whiteboards. Informal brainstorming rooms are distributed among cubes. Coffee and copy

Netscape Communications

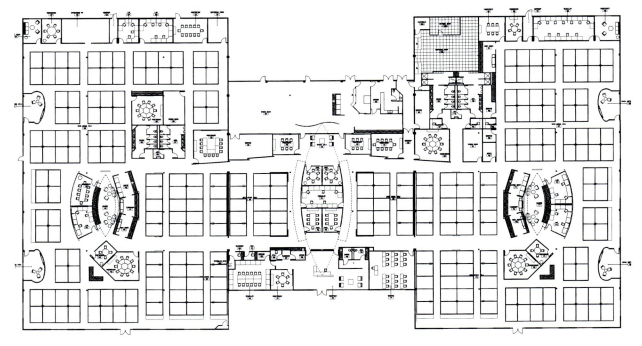

Facing page
A curving shape defines a football-shaped seating area, which is accessible from both ends of the space. The lounge is strategically located next to coffee and fax areas, with conference rooms clustered around it. The space is large enough to accommodate a large team, but comfortable enough for a one-person quiet time. The two-level carpeted bench sits opposite a floor-to-ceiling, wall to wall whiteboard. The curved ceiling component has aluminum trim, which is pulled away from the ceiling, and punched skylights in the roof bring natural light into core of the building.

The plan of Building 14 reveals that this 67,000-square-foot floor was once three separate units, with concrete shear walls between them. The renovation cut openings as large as possible to create an open quality and logical circulation. Staff support areas enclose lounges, making services accessible while screening noise from the office areas. Labs and conference rooms line perimeter to further segregate noise and activity. The distinctive football shape, appearing as a void in the lounges, appears as a solid element of labs and conference rooms at the center of the building. Circulation flows around the curves, connecting the entry lobby with the cafeteria/meeting room.

The reception area in Building 14 features a custom reception desk and inexpensive materials. The space is surrounded by visitor amenities so they never have to enter the secured research and development space. A frosted glass wall is behind the desk, with a slice of vision glass at the center to provide both illumination and visual communication with people in the adjoining conference room.

rooms form service centers which segregate noisy work from quiet work. Gensler designed and documented these buildings within a ten-week period and construction was completed after only fourteen weeks.

For Building SV-1—a massive, two-level 137,000-square-foot structure—the Gensler designers combined large training facilities, finance, sales and administrative offices in one cohesive facility. Meeting the design challenge in this multi-function building meant re-using the existing acoustic tile ceilings (which remained intact throughout the construction process and were incorporated into the final design vocabulary), the two-by-four lights, and mechanical distribution systems, for both budgetary and scheduling concerns. **The groups occupying this facility make extensive use of multi-sized conference spaces and require numerous file rooms and larger break and lunch rooms.** Gensler suggested that administrative employees would benefit from the same blending of work, decompression, and relaxation spaces that engineers enjoy. Like the other Netscape interiors projects, this facility was also on the tightest of schedules. The Gensler team planned the space within eight weeks and construction was completed in about fourteen weeks.

The Gensler team also designed a small Netscape retail store for the Mountain View campus. This shop, which sells software products and branded merchandise, was designed with Netscape's themes of navigation and exploration in mind, including a floor which suggests ocean waters, walls which fade from daylight to night, panels of back-lit "stars," and nighttime sky pinpointed with halogen. The popular and successful shop provides visitors and employees with merchandise to identify themselves with Netscape. Again, the challenge was the schedule: the store was designed in about three days, documented in approximately two weeks, and constructed in less than a month, just in time for holiday shopping.

Gensler's collaboration with Netscape's business and engineering management has established standards for space, typical arrangements for labs, data frames, group work areas, project rooms, and standard work stations for various types of jobs. **Gensler also helped Netscape address the issue of open office plans versus private offices in their efforts to eliminate hierarchies in the workplace and establish an egalitarian, team-oriented workforce that is more in keeping with their corporate culture.**

Costs throughout the Netscape facilities were managed by using inexpensive materials in exciting, unexpected ways. Throughout these diverse facilities, creativity was fostered by blurring the traditional distinctions among individual workspaces, team-work space, and lounge and support areas. By designing generic engineering and administrative spaces, Gensler accelerated their own design process and the subsequent construction while giving Netscape flexibility. This design philosophy also increased the flexibility of the spaces without hindering innovative thinking (employees can move files documenting months of work and research simply by plugging into a new connector, for example).

Netscape is a young fast-growing, company and Gensler has created a workplace that reflects and nurtures the organization's exiting culture. The Gensler team established an innovative environment that hosts small and large, generic and specific, and individual and shared spaces. **Through all the projects, the guiding principle was a blurring of the boundries among work, decompression, and relaxation spaces as the team explored new notions of flexibility and process appropriate to an on-line workplace.** By mid-1998 the Gensler team will have completed an additional 250,000 square feet in four buildings. Netscape's Internet expertise, coupled with Gensler's ability to plan functional work environments, have defined a new notion of flexibility, a notion that will continue to inform the development of the workplace.

Plan Building 15. Circulation is clearly defined with built elements, positioned for maximum accessibility to all inhabitants. The strenght of the furniture system is maximized by keeping the bulk of the floor space open and unencumhered by permanent construction.

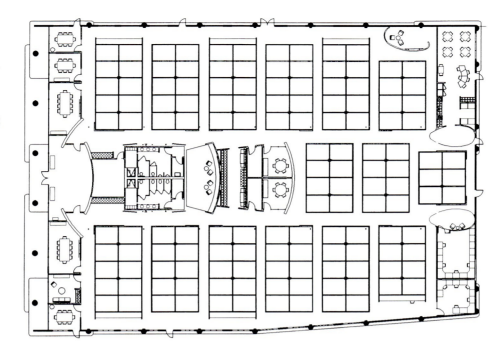

Netscape believes taking a break can be as creative as sitting at a desk, and people who work long hours need a fun space in which to relax. An entire wall surface covered with velcro is an easy target for a collection of toys which Netscape people can throw in their breaktime. The opposite wall features a long curving white wall, positioned to capture random thoughts and burgeoning ideas.

Building 14. This view looks down aisle toward the checkerboard design element. In order to accentuate the plane of panels along the clearly defined circulation path, the panels are pulled apart with fluorescent lights placed between the panels to give a sense of light. To the right, six-foot-square windows equipped with outsized venetian aluminum blinds look into large conference rooms. At the end of the image, a black stripe indicates the top of a concrete wall that Gensler cut above the ceiling grid in order to give the space a sense of continuity.

This image of the main aisle of Building 15 looking toward lounge and lab area demonstrates how Gensler addressed the significant issue of the large scale and 15-foot-high ceiling of the building. The panels, which have wing walls at locations of high activity, are used to help buffer workers from noise and distractions.

Plan of SV-1. The plan emphasizes a clear circulation system, critical on a 65,000-square-foot floorplate. The distribution of meeting and support spaces creates smaller areas which humanize the scale of the vast space. An existing exit corridor separates the open office from training rooms.

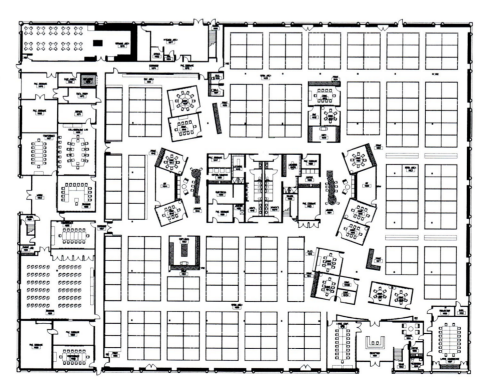

Lounge area of 137,000-square-foot administration office space. The lounges feature a large seating area and banquettes that accommodate overflow at lunch.

Interior of the store incorporates the navigational theme of the Netscape image; water represented by the blue tile floor, stars as seen in the black ceiling which features small light elements, and land (modular display pieces). All display pieces are aluminum trimmed with clamps to attach shelves.

The Netscape General Store, created in a six-week time frame, is located in a former conference room. Visitors to the Customer Briefing Center, located across the large, landscaped seating area, have direct access to the store.

Businesses are ever-more competitive, more focused on strategic positioning, and more eager to find ways to leverage higher levels of productivity and performance. The Gensler designers are aware of the forces of change affecting the way people work and, consequently, how office environments should be planned and designed. Gensler is involved in a design process that develops strategic workplace environments that are flexible and adaptable in order to facilitate the dynamism of the contemporary business world and address its ever-changing needs.

However the business world might label an organization's transformation—re-engineering, repositioning, downsizing, or right-sizing—these new strategies have compelled workplace designers to ask new questions and work more closely with clients to reconsider the way space is used. Gensler has found that organizations are most effective when space design closely aligns with, and reinforces, the occupant's organizational culture, work process requirements, and strategic direction.

Business organizations are required to adapt to a constantly evolving set of issues and challenges, and designers understand that every project arises from a compelling business decision. Gensler implements a project strategy that responds uniquely, whether clients are facing an expiring lease, a recent merger with another company, or a need to attract the best talent in their industry. In order to establish clear guidelines for understanding these issues and define a course of action that properly influences the development of the architecture of the workplace,

Workplace Task Force

Gensler established a Workplace Task Force. The Workplace Task Force is an internal think tank focused on the development of expertise in order to guide the Gensler designers in new workplace strategies.

Gensler has worked with Gap, Inc. since the time both companies were formed. Although Gensler had experience designing the Gap's retail facilities, the project for their new San Bruno, California, corporate headquarters represented a new challenge for the designers. For this project, Gensler collaborated with environmental architects William McDonough & Partners, a firm noted for its sustainable building design. The building and interior design will respond to a number of environmental and social issues. The objective was to create a sense of "neighborhood" within the space, maximize the use of natural light, underscore an awareness of the outside environment, and employ a limited vocabulary of design elements and finishes. One of Gensler's challenges was to consolidate the Gap staff into teaming clusters in order to reinforce the collaborative spirit. The entire facility was designed with raised flooring to obtain the greatest flexibility, and each workspace was provided with individual climate control for maximum comfort.

Private offices, research laboratories, and collaborative work spaces comprise the new home of AT&T Labs, a 245,000 square-foot building in Florham Park, New Jersey. The Gensler team of designers and planners selectively renovated the existing facility to accommodate a portion of the Research and Development division following AT&T's

AT&T Research Labs, Florham Park, NJ
The "Slate Room" is a designated space where teams of mathematicians can meet for easy collaboration. The 28-foot-diameter hexagonal room features a continuous surround of floor-to-ceiling slate blackboards with ottoman-type seating towards the center. Gensler designed the ceiling to be as high as possible, with indirect lighting. The room is surrounded by coffee room, copy/print space and files.

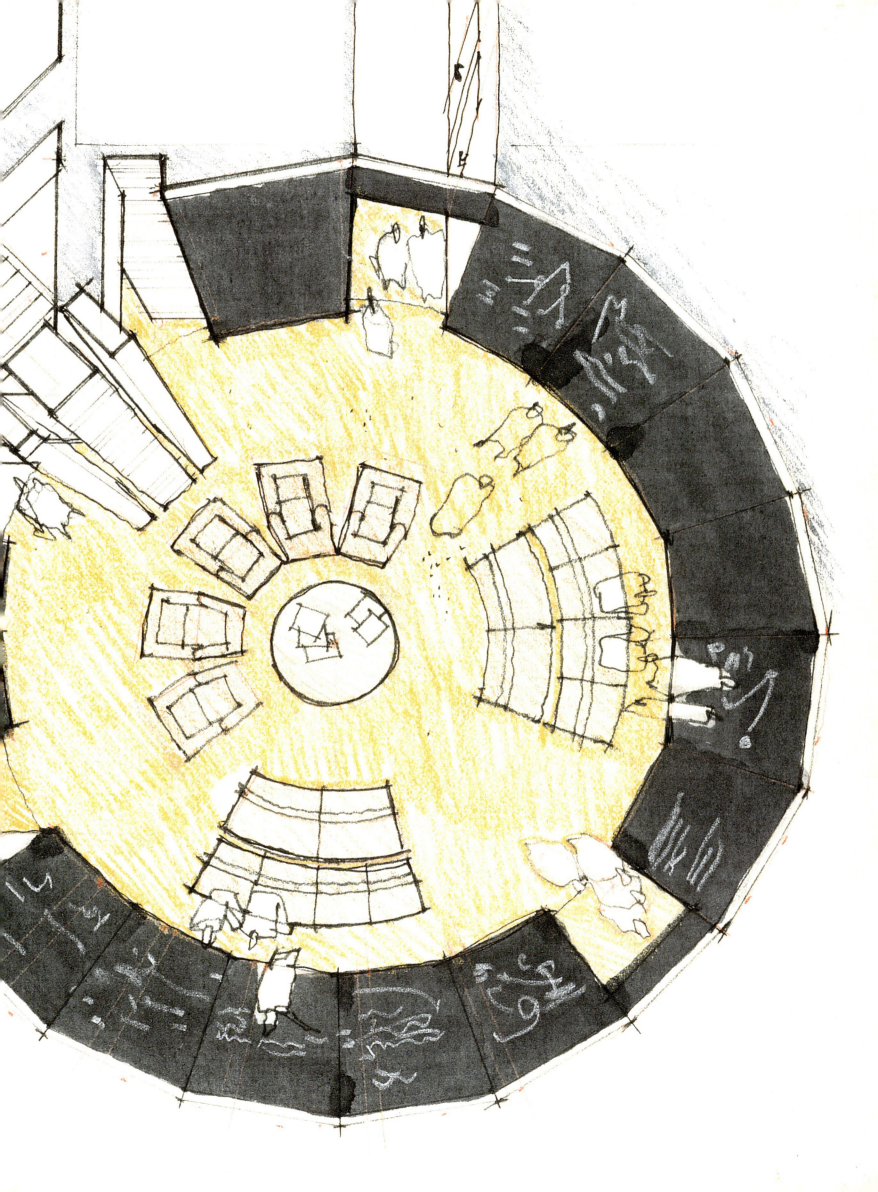

restructuring. Taking advantage of existing conditions, Gensler designers created a high-performance work environment that balances a variety of functions. To highlight the core of AT&T Labs, the Gensler team designed a hexagonal-shaped research space for mathematicians. Aptly named the "Slate Room," due to the mathematicians' preference for using chalk and natural slate writing surfaces, the room is prominently situated at the head of the main stair leading from the entrance atrium. The "Slate Room" features soft seating in the center surrounded by slate blackboards that reach from floor to ceiling, illustrating the mathematicians' labors and allowing for the performance-like communication of ideas and concepts.

After working with a major consulting firm for ten years, Gensler was asked to re-explore their work environment and processes, and to adjust the space and the ways in which the occupants interact to help the company better meet their goals. Using the firm's New York office as a pilot, Gensler determined that the current workspace wasn't promoting the team-driven, interactive nature of the firm's business as successfully as it could. For example, consultants were not located near partners and other resources, and communication and mentoring opportunities were hindered by this distance. As a response to this situation, Gensler organized the floorplate into clusters with enough space for eight to ten consultants and a partner/mentor. Each team was provided with a dedicated resource area consisting of four team assistants and graphics people who are critical in assembling client deliverables, as well as a dedicated team room in which the consultants spend over 50 percent of their time. In addition, each consultant has a private workplace consisting of a seven-by-ten-foot module with a sliding door. Rather than the more traditional reception/conference areas found on other floors, the consultants on the project opted to include a pool table, monitors for viewing CNN, and a coffee bar and international newspaper area to further enhance consultant interaction.

In anticipation of their move to a new headquarters space, Union Pacific Resources Company (UPR) launched a project to consider the ways in which the work environment could be a more effective tool in helping UPR reach its business strategy goals. Gensler began the project by interpreting UPR's operational requirements, cultural behavior, and strategic business goals, and translating them into a physical work environment representative of UPR's changing work practices.

A highly interactive process was developed to understand UPR's current and anticipated working culture, styles, practices, and technology. An internal task force, with participants representing nearly every area of UPR, worked with Gensler to develop the new environment, and was also on hand to test various concepts and recommendations throughout the design process. Gensler conducted four levels of research: workshops, interviews, focus groups, and surveys. These activities were selected as part of a strategy to promote the sharing of information throughout the company and to reinforce many of the changes already underway. The data collected from the research indicated a series of emerging trends and identified areas that would require more research.

Gensler was retained by General Motors to assist with the relocation of GM's global headquarters to the two million-square-foot Renaissance Center in downtown Detroit, Michigan. The project represents the collaboration of various groups from several locations to create an efficient corporate decision-making environment. Gensler provided planning and design guidelines for the company's facilities worldwide as well as full-scale interior design services for this global headquarters. The Gensler design replaced scores of private offices with open workstations, team areas, and common floor plans, and transformed GM's traditional workplace by removing walls to encourage teamwork and give employees—not their managers—the best views of Detroit and its waterfront. Realizing that GM wanted an interactive, team-based work environment that would be flexible enough to change with the needs

Workplace Design Process

Union Pacific Resources Workplace Design Process chart. In anticipation of their move into new headquarters space, UPR launched a project to look at the ways in which the work environment can be a more effective tool in helping the company reach its business strategy goals. Gensler began the project by assisting UPR in interpreting the company's operational requirements, cultural behaviors, and strategic business goals. The next step was to translate these needs and goals into a physical work environment representative of their changing culture and work practices, now and in the future.

General Motors Corporation
Gensler was retained by General Motors to assist with the relocation of the world's largest manufacturing corporation to its two million-square-foot Global Headquarters at the Renaissance Center in downtown Detroit. The project represents a consolidation of various groups from several locations to create an efficient corporate decision-making environment. Open workstations, team areas, and common floor plans replace scores of private offices Initially, new office concepts were developed and implemented to support the company's business plan, which called for flexible office space adaptable to different work processes. Gensler's recommendations for the Common Systems Initiative included development of space standards, furniture standards, universal planning, interior architectural performance criteria, and facilities management approaches. General Motors challenged the Gensler team to design an interactive, team-based work environment. Gensler responded with an approach that enables flexibility, while lowering the costs associated with the churn of employee relocations. The result is a workplace that gives General Motors the functional tools they need to get their product out quickly.

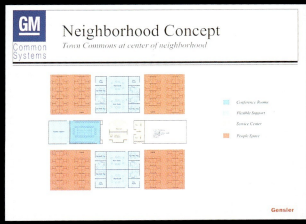
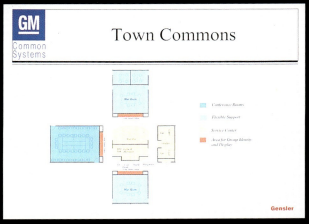
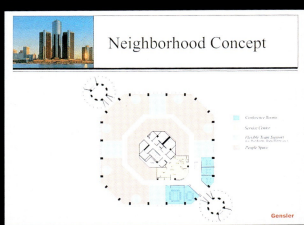
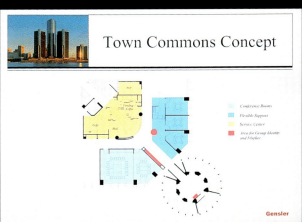

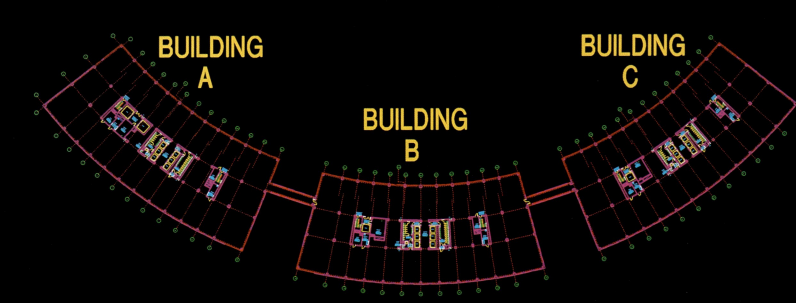

Internal Revenue Service, New Carrolton, Maryland
The GSA commissioned Gensler to provide space planning and design services for three new IRS buildings, totaling 1.3 million square feet. This was Gensler's first significant project for the GSA and demonstrates how the US government is incorporating innovative planning concepts into its work environments and how these strategies can be successful, even on a significantly large-scale level. Following the Universal Plan, Gensler planned the IRS divisions into 24 floors of office space. The employee populations for the buildings are 4,444.

of its business, Gensler came up with a flexible approach that still kept the costs associated with the churn of employee relocations low. The result is a workplace that supports General Motors' corporate goals.

The GSA commissioned Gensler to provide space planning and design services for three new IRS buildings, totaling 1.3 million square feet. This project, Gensler's first significant one for the GSA, demonstrates how the United States government is incorporating innovative planning concepts into its work environments and how these strategies can be successful, even on a very large-scale level. Gensler incorporated a universal planning concept and placed the IRS divisions within twenty-four floors of office space. With 4,444 employees in each building, the typical floor houses 182 employees, 90 percent of which are in open plan workstations. The IRS had pre-existing workstation and office standards which were used in developing the planning concept. The final selections were made after the space planning stage, so all furniture specifications were generic, conformed to GSA standards, and were appropriate for bidding.

When the Gensler designers were retained by QVC to design their West Chester, Pennsylvania, facility they quickly learned that their new client was a virtual shopping mall that never closes, with a volume of two customers per second, 24 hours a day, seven days a week, and telecasts of themed programs viewed by over sixty-three million households in the United States everyday.

Gensler designed a new office space, production studio, storage, cafeteria, public areas, and studio tour component as part of the adaptive reuse of an existing 550,000 square-foot warehouse and light manufacturing facility. For this project, Gensler utilized designers from their New York team to plan and design QVC's office component, their Los Angeles office to focus on the broadcasting facilities, and their San Francisco office to design the studio tour graphics. The program involved base building upgrades, reworking the main entry to provide a

QVC, West Chester, PA
The QVC electronic retailing headquarters/broadcasting project is an adaptive reuse of an existing warehouse and light industrial manufacturing facility. The office portion will establish an atmosphere that is non-traditional, warm but high-tech, energetic and forward-thinking. All staff members will be located in one building in order to reinforce a spirit of collaboration and innovation.

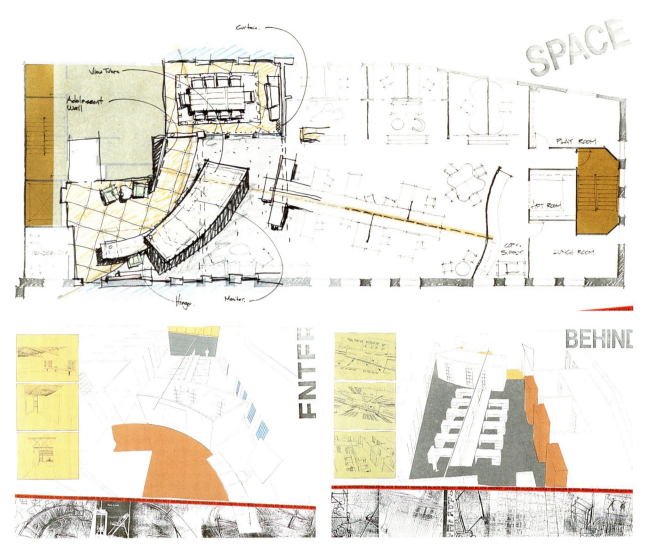

Black Rocket, San Francisco
Top of page. Given the time and money constraints, Black Rocket initially asked Gensler to reuse as much of the exiting tenant improvements in the 4,000-square-foot space as possible.

Above left. The design process was an eclectic mix of concept storyboards from Black Rocket, work pattern diagrams from Gensler, and material mock-ups from Zack Architecture.

Above right. All schemes challenged Black Rocket to determine how few enclosed spaces they required to do their work. In this diagram only collaborative areas were enclosed, and all staff sat in an open central area.

Below. The highly interactive design process created a completely different scheme every week until a strong, simple concept emerged. Below, private workspaces ring a central zone housing the firm library, workstations, and layout areas. A masking tape and cardboard mock-up of this concept was tested by Black Rocket staff prior to plan approval.

T. Rowe Price Associates, Inc., Owings Mills, Maryland

1. The client's new corporate campus will serve as the focus of operations, telephone service, technological support and systems development groups for varying departments within the company. Four buildings of 100,000 - 120,000 square feet each are ultimately planned for the 32-acre site and will be developed in phases. The buildings are to be of comparable size and treatment, but with some individuality.
2. The buildings will house groups that are heavily technology-reliant. The building sizes, shapes, disposition of core elements, and overall costs are also required to be comparable to those of other class "A" office buildings in the area.
3. Gensler developed the program for user spaces and summarized building design criteria for use by the building architect. On the interior, Gensler designed, produced construction documents, and provided construction administration. The facilities were designed for specific workplace needs but suitable for sublet should planned expansion occur more slowly than planned.
4. Project goals included: provide high level of technological connectivity and infrastructure; adapt to change in business activities; support time-critical business activities; and enhance employee activity in pleasant business-like atmosphere.
5. Gensler created a floorplate that allows for workstation clusters to adapt to three sizes in any location. Floorplate design allows for multiple divisions of space.
6. Workstations feature best-technology: sized for equipment, ambient lighting, and standard connections for power/communications.

DreamWorks Animation Campus, Glendale, California
Top of page. Plan. Based on the belief that employees, particularly animators, are happier working in the comfort of their homes, the primary strategy in designing the animation campus was to create an inviting, comfortable workplace with a residential feel. This ambiance is reinforced through colors, materials, and space layout. Bringing the residential elements of the exterior inside, arcades become corridors, courtyards become living rooms, and archways will continue to manifest a non-corporate look.
An unusually large number of private offices will be available for the animators who typically seek solitude while designing.
Above. Concept. Living rooms furnished with overstuffed sofas and attractive coffee tables, surrounded by unadorned walls for storyboard viewing, are places in which to meet and collaborate. Pitch rooms will contain castered chairs and movable storyboard props as opposed to the typical conference room table, to facilitate dynamic sessions. Coffee areas, stocked with complimentary snacks, will be open around the clock to the entire staff.

handicap accessible drop-off, new canopy, reception lobby, and a new curtain wall to enclose the office space. New mechanical systems were integrated with existing services to allow for incremental growth. In addition to architecture and interior design, Gensler also provided all departmental identification graphics and themed environmental graphics.

Black Rocket, is a twenty-two person advertising agency that needed to fit into a small 4,000 square-foot Port of San Francisco space with unique warehouse and waterfront characteristics. Like building a ship in a bottle, Gensler's design for Black Rocket reduced the activities of an advertising firm down to its fundamental functional essence.

A "Creative Cloister" was created by arranging small private spaces for creative work around a central space whose walls acted as the company library. This central open room kept the visual character of the spacious warehouse volume intact, and maintained unobstructed views of the waterfront outside.

During the early stages of the Black Rocket project, Gensler partnered in a unique collaboration with Zack Architecture, a design-build firm, and the collaborators envisioned the concept of creating an interior office space as flexible as furniture. The only permanent items in the design are twelve radiating walls and mechanical duct work. If Black Rocket moves, all the other elements in the space can be unbolted, moved, and rebuilt elsewhere.

The objective of T. Rowe Price Associates is to help individuals achieve their financial goals. Toward this end, the firm offers investors comprehensive financial planning information and the tools to make confident investment decisions. The firm's objective for developing their new corporate campus in Owings Mills, Maryland, was to have the campus serve as the focus of operations, communications service, technological support, and systems development groups for various departments. The planned thirty-two-acre site hosts four buildings with approximately 600,000 square feet of space.

Gensler developed the program for the user spaces. The team worked with the base building architects to summarize design criteria, including the building core and shell, site development, interior space configuration, and engineering requirements. The facilities were designed for this specific workplace, but are also suitable for sublet should planned expansion occur more slowly than anticipated.

Gensler and Steven Ehrlich Architects were commissioned by DreamWorks SKG to produce the master plan and design of a new animation campus to support the television and feature film production facilities. DreamWorks SKG is Hollywood's first all new film and television studio to be built in sixty years. The plan and design take advantage of this unique opportunity to create the optimum new seating configuration for the studio of the future.

Located on a thirteen-acre triangular site in Glendale, California, adjacent to the Los Angeles River, the animation campus will offer a unique environment for the animation industry. The 330,000 square-foot campus consists of five low-rise buildings and a parking structure interconnected through arcades, verandas, and bridges. The exterior design utilizes Mediterranean styling and warm hues, abundant arches, and lush courtyards. A manmade river will meander through the project, flowing under two of the buildings, following the path of a natural arroyo that was once part of the Los Angeles River.

For this project, Gensler drew upon its extensive experience in interior design and planning to help DreamWorks SKG define the physical and functional requirements for the animation group's future home. Based on the belief that employees, particularly animators, are happier working in the comfort of their homes, the primary strategy in designing the campus was to create an inviting, comfortable workplace with a residential feel. Bringing the residential elements of the exterior inside, arcades become corridors, courtyards become "living rooms," and archways continue to manifest a non-corporate look. A very large number of private offices will be available for the animators who typically seek solitude while designing, and, just as at home, the space provides a common room for "family" gatherings in which to meet and collaborate.

In the mid-1980s, EDS established a strategy that led to the development of their Plano, Texas, campus. Over the years, that strategy has not fundamentally changed, and EDS was eager to know what additions might be needed to accommodate the demands of the current market. Gensler was asked to participate in a Real Estate Strategic Alignment Project, focusing on EDS' campus in Plano. The purpose of the assignment was to determine whether EDS' real estate strategy was aligned with its business strategy. The project had two objectives: to perform a "sanity check" on the real estate strategies that brought EDS to its current situation, and to develop a strategy for the future. Gensler's review of EDS' situation indicated that the company's performance exceeded current industry benchmarks such as operating costs and square footage per person. Gensler divided the real estate strategies into three sections—land, business, and workplace—resulting in several important recommendations. One recommendation was that EDS utilize a kit-of-parts approach with freestanding furniture and less panel dependency in order to promote openness, communication, and incorporate user-oriented solutions while maintaining existing densities.

Gensler worked with Armstrong World Industries to consolidate all facilities into the Lancaster, Pennsylvania, campus. For the first phase of this project, Gensler was involved in a master planning and facilities analysis of 800,000 square feet of existing property. The Gensler team helped develop use strategies, budgets, and timing for seven existing buildings in order to maximize the value of the total portfolio. Additionally, Gensler is renovating what was the corporation's design and development building to serve as a "campus center," providing Armstrong employees with a common place to gather and interact daily.

Gensler's Workplace Task Force examines and analyzes the significant issues at the core of progressive change in the business world. Their comprehensive network offers specialized knowledge and integrated thinking about balance, integration, flexibility and performance in today's workplace. The Gensler teams of architects, designers, and planners are committed to developing the architecture of the new workplace. They have emerged into an extraordinary field of activity that goes well beyond the mere organization and planning of interior spaces. These designers are involved in a detailed process of before, during, and after stages, each with its specific challenges. Today's successful workplace designers have their finger on the pulse of business activities and can anticipate not only stylistic trends, but changes in corporate culture, technology, work patterns, and the quality of work life in general.

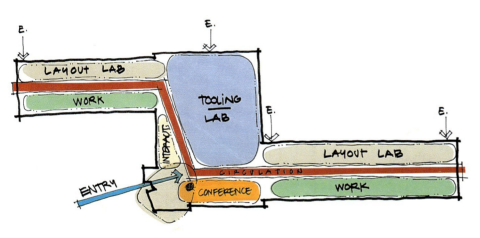

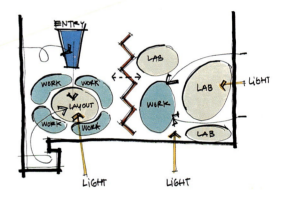

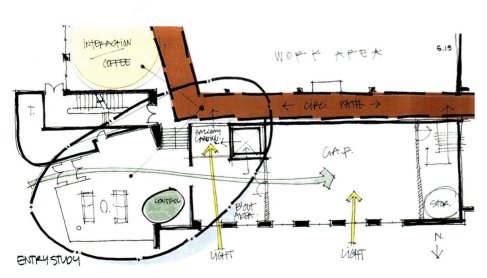

Armstrong World Industries. Gensler was retained by Armstrong to develop a new administration building in support of its efforts to consolidate multiple facilities to a single "Innovation Center". Increasing synergies among all functions from product styling to finance was the primary goal. The project grew to encompass almost every existing buliding as well as two new buildings on the 250-acre campus. Integral to both the new and renovated buildings is a need to provide flexibility while addressing the specialized needs of individual organizations. Gensler worked closely with leaders from each of Armstrong's main product organizations to ensure the right product contributes to the overall solution for each project. Each organization within Armstrong worked with Gensler to identify their specific needs and then develop diagrams of their work processes. The most complex were encountered in the design of the Research & Development Zone for the campus. Beginning from these simple but accurate diagrams, concept solutions were tested against the realities of the existing building's constraints. The new work zones within the building provide opportunities for collaboration, at intersections between design, development and reserch areas. Each of these is designed to accommodate change through a "kit of parts" designed to specifically support processes today and tomorrow.

Credits

**Apple Computer, Inc.
De Anza 3 Campus**

Consultants:
Acoustical
Charles M. Salter Associates, Inc.
Audiovisual
Robert M. Morris, Jr. Architect AIA
Code
Rolf Jensen & Associates, Inc.
Construction Management
Rudolph and Sletten, Inc.
Electrical Engineer
Marion, Cerbatos & Tomasi
Fire/Life Safety
Rolf Jensen & Associates, Inc.
Food Service
Cini-Little International
General Contractor
Rudolph and Sletten, Inc.
Landscape
Hargreaves Associates
Lighting
Horton-Lees Lighting Design, Inc.
Mechanical Engineer
Bouillon, Christoffersen & Schairer
Plumbing
George Greene Company
Structural Engineer
Putterman-Davis

Photography
Jon Miller, Hedrich Blessing;
Chas McGrath

**Apple Computer, Inc.
U.S. Customer Service Center**

Associate Architect:
The Bommarito Group

Consultants:
General Contractor
Faulkner Contruction Company
Landscape
Evergreen Landscaping
MEP
Hendrix & Myers

Photography
Paul Bardagjy

**Apple Computer, Inc.
Research and Development**

Base Building Architect:
Hellmuth, Obata and Kassabaum, Inc.

Consultants:
General Contractor
Rudolph and Sletten, Inc.
Lighting
S.L. Auerbach and Associates

Photography
Chas McGrath

**Becton Dickinson
Immunocytometry Systems**

Consultants:
Construction Management
Fluor Daniel
Electrical Engineer
The Engineering Enterprise
General Contractors
Hodgson Construction
Nico Construction
Lighting
Horton-Lees Lighting Design, Inc.
Mechanical Engineer
Gayner Engineers
Laboratory
McLellan & Copenhagen
Structural Engineer
Nishkian & Associates

Photography
Nick Merrick,
Hedrich Blessing

**Chevron, Corporation
575 Market Street**
Base Building Architect:
Hertzka & Knowles
(Completed - 1975)

Consultants:
Electrical
The Engineering Enterprise
Mechanical
Gayner Engineers
Structural
Forell/Elsesser Engineers, Inc.
Landscape
Hellmuth, Obata & Kassabaum
Audiovisual
EIS
Food Service
The Marshall Associates, Inc.
Lighting (Executive Floors)
Horton-Lees Lighting Design, Inc.
Lighting (Lobby, Garden & Conference Center)
The Engineering Enterprise
Accoustical
Charles M. Salter Associates, Inc.
Art Consultant
ArtSource

Photography
Chas McGrath

Columbia/HCA Call Center

Consultants:
Call Center Management
ERS
General Contractor
Austin Commercial, Inc.
MEP
BCER Consulting Engineers

Photography
Paul Bardagjy

Enron Corp
Base Building Architect:
Lloyd Jones & Fillpot

Consultants:
Code
Rolf Jensen & Associates, Inc.
Food Service
Szabo Food Service
General Contractor
Partners Construction Company
Lighting
Theo Kondos Associates
Mechanical/Electrical
I.A. Naman & Associates, Inc.
Security
Sako & Associates
Structural Engineer
Ellisor & Tanner
Telecommunications
Southwestern Bell Telecom

Photography
Nick Merrick,
Hedrich Blessing

Epson America, Inc.

Consultants:
Audiovisual
Cibola
Electrical Engineer
Syska & Hennessy
General Contractor
Shimizu Corporation
Landscape
Takeo Uesugi & Associates
Lighting
Patrick Quigley & Associates

Mechanical Engineer
Syska & Hennessy
Pool/Fountain Design
Waterscape Technologies
Structural
Teo Otova & Associates

Photography
Michael Arden; Marco Lorenzetti, Hedrich Blessing

**Federal Reserve System
Board of Governors
Boardroom**

Consultants:
Audiovisual
Presentation Planning, Inc.
Chair Manufacturer & Refurbisher
David Edward
Contractor
Rand Construction
Masonry
American Mosaic
Millwork
Enterprise Woodcraft
Drywall
Hayles & Howe
Wall Fabric/Rug Manufacturer
Scalamandre
Wood Flooring
Exquisite Floor

Photography
Walter Smalling

Davis Polk & Wardwell

Base Building Architect:
Skidmore, Owings & Merrill
(1992)

Consultants:
Acoustical
Shen Milsom & Wilke, Inc.
Audiovisual
Smith Meeker Engineering
Code/Filing
Jerome S. Gillman Consulting Architect PC
Construction Management
Bennis & Reissman
Design Consultant
Eva Ching
General Contractor
A.J. Contracting Company, Inc.
Graphic Design
Vignelli & Associates
Lighting
Cline, Bettridge, Bernstein Lighting Design Inc.
MEP
FMC Associates
Millwork
John Langenbacher Co., Inc.
Nordic
Rimi Woodcraft Corp.
Security
Integrated Access Systems
Structural Engineer
Severud & Associates
Telecommunications
AT&T
Vertical Transportation
Jenkins & Huntington, Inc.
Translogic Corp.

Photography
Nick Merrick,
Hedrich Blessing

**Goldman, Sachs & Co.
85 Broad St.**

Base Building Architect:
Skidmore, Owings & Merrill

Consultants:
Acoustical
Robert A. Hansen Associates, Inc.

Code
Cole-Gilman Associates
Construction Management
Lehrer McGovern Bovis, Inc.
Filing
Metropolis Consulting
General Contractor
Lehrer McGovern Bovis, Inc.
Lighting
Cline, Bettridge, Bernstein Lighting Design Inc.
Jerry Kugler Associates, Inc.
MEP
Flack & Kurtz
Syska & Hennessy, Inc.
Structural Engineer
Weidlinger Associates

Photography
Jaime Ardiles-Arce;
Marco Lorenzetti,
Hedrich Blessing

**Goldman, Sachs & Co.
One New York Plaza**

Photography
Marco Lorenzetti,
Hedrich Blessing

**Goldman, Sachs
International Ldt.,
London**

Base Building Architect:
Kohn Pedersen Fox Associates
Associate Architect:
Elsom Pack & Roberts Partnership
YRM Interiors

Consultants:
Acoustical
Shen Milsom & Wilke, Inc.
Audivisual
Shen Milsom & Wilke, Inc.
Construction Management
Trench Farrow & Partners
Cost
Bernard Williams Associates
Food Service
Beer Associates
General Contractor
Taylor Woodrow Management Contracting Ltd.
Lighting
YRM Engineers
Designed Architectural Lighting Co., Ltd.
Mechanical/Electrical
Flack & Kurtz
Security
Schiff & Associates, Inc.
Structural Engineer
Ove Arup & Partners

Photography
Jaime Ardiles-Arce

HarperCollins Publishers

Base Building Architect:
Hellmuth, Obata & Kassabaum
(Completed - 1979)

Consultants:
Acoustical Ceiling Tile
Carlos Interior Systems, Inc.
Design-Build Electrical Subcontractor
Cupertino Electric
The Engineering Enterprise
Fire/Life Safety
Pribuss Engineering, Inc.
General Contractor
BCCI Construction Company
Muralist
Ann Field
Lighting
Horton-Lees Lighting Design, Inc.

Design-Build Mechanical Subcontractor
Linford Air & Refrigeration Co.
Security
Metro Security Systems
Structural Engineer
Structural Design Engineers
Telecommunications
COMSUL, Inc.

Photography
Chas McGrath

Hoffmann-La Roche

Base Building Architect:
The Hillier Group

Consultants:
Acoustical
Acentech Incorporated
Audiovisual
Smith-Meeker Engineering
Color Consultant
Donald Kaufman Color
Construction Management
Gilbane Building Company
Lighting
Hillmann/DiBernardo
Mechanical Engineer
R.G. Vanderweil Consulting Engineers
Security
Schiff & Associates, Inc.
Structural Engineer
Cantor Seinuk Group
Telecommunications
CS Technology

Photography
Peter Aaron; Marco Lorenzetti, Hedrich Blessing

MasterCard International

Base Building Architect:
I.M. Pei & Partners

Consultants:
Acoustical
Cerami and Associates, Inc.
Art
Vick Corporate Art Advisors
Audiovisual
Smith Meeker Engineering
Communications
CS Technology
Construction Management
Structure Tone, Inc.
Bennis & Reissman
Filing
D.C. Turano, Inc.
Fitness
Fitness Systems
Food Service
Beer Associates
Furniture
Coro Services Inc.
General Contractor
Structure Tone, Inc.
Lighting
Hillmann/DiBernardo
Mechanical/Electrical
JB&B
Security
Schiff & Associates, Inc.
Structural Engineer
Severud & Associates
Surveying
J. Bain & Associates

Photography
Peter Paige

MCI Communications

Consultants:
Acoustical
David L. Adams Associates, Inc.
Audiovisual
Video Dynamics
Civil
KLH Engineering, Inc.
Food Service
Thomas Ricca Associates
General Contractor
Weitz Cohen Construction Co.
Geotechnical
CTL/Thompson
Landscape
Civitas, Inc.
Lighting
ABS Mechanical Consultants, Inc.
Jerry Kugler Associates
Mechanical/Electrical
ABS Mechanical Consultants, Inc.
Project Management
Woziwodzki Group
Structural Engineer
Martin & Martin

Photography
Marco Lorenzetti,
Hedrich Blessing,
Thorney Lieberman

Morrison & Foerster

Base Building Architect:
Hoover Associates

Consultants:
Structural Engineer
RMJ

Photography
Chas McGrath,
Marco Lorenzetti,
Hedrich Blessing

Netscape Communications

Consultants:
Electrical Engineer
Design Electric
General Contractor
Rudolph and Sletten, Inc.
Mechanical Engineer
Air Systems, Inc.
Project Management
FaciliCorp

Photography
Paul Warchol

Prudential Insurance Company Of America

Base Building Architect:
A. C. Martin & Associates

Consultants:
Electrical Engineer
Fischbach & Moore
General Contractor
Robert McKee Construction
Mechanical Engineer
F. B. Gardner

Photography
Toshi Yoshimi, Paul Bielenberg

RepublicBank of Houston

Base Building Architect:
Philip Johnson and John Burgee
Associate Architect:
Kendall Heeton Associates

Consultants:
Art
Sowder & Associates
Audiovisual
Pran, Inc.
Engineering Consultants
I.A. Naman & Associates
Lookwood, Andrews & Newman, Inc.
General Contractor
Turner Construction
Lighting
Marlene Lee
Structural
CBM

Photography
Chas McGrath

Taylor + Smith

Consultants:
Audiovisual
J & S Communications
Construction
Marek Brothers Systems Inc.
Electrical Engineer
Mid-West Electric Company
General Contractor
LTB Interior Constructors Inc.
Graphics
GraphTec, Inc.
Mechanical Engineer
Graves Mechanical
Millwork
Johns and Hausmann
Structural Engineer
Walter P. Moore & Associates, Inc.

Photography
Nash Baker

Union Bank of Switzerland

Base Building Architect:
Emery Roth & Sons, P.C.

Consultants:
Acoustical
Cerami Associates
Art
Dr. Ziba DeWeck
Scott Burton/Artist
General Contractor
Ramco Alterations Co., Inc.
Lighting
Cline, Bettridge, Bernstein Lighting Design, Inc.
Mechanical/Electrical
Edwards & Zuck, P.E.
Millwork
Rimi Woodcraft Corp.
Eckert Johnson
Structural Engineer
The Office of James Ruderman

Photography
Jaime Ardiles-Arce

Cover photography

Epson America, Inc.
Marco Lorenzetti,
Hedrich Blessing

Additional Photography Credits

Page 7, Consolidated Freightways
Jaime Ardiles-Arce
Page 7, DMB&B
Marco Lorenzetti,
Hedrich Blessing
Page 8, Bank of America
Paul Bielenberg
Page 8, BankBoston
Robert Miller
Page 9, Gensler San Francisco
Chas McGrath
Page 9, Gensler Washington, D.C.
Walter Smalling
Page 11, Pennzoil Company
Richard Payne
Page 12, Mobil Oil Corporation
Mark Ross
Page 13, Mobil Oil Corporation
Mark Ross
Page 14, Wachtell, Lipton, Rosen & Katz
Marco Lorenzetti
Page 15, Cravath, Swaine & Moore
Nick Merrick, Hedrich Blessing
Page 16, Gensler New York
Nick Merrick
Page 18, Baker & Botts
Toshi Yoshimi
Page 18, Society Bank
Nick Merrick
Page 20, Capital Bank
Nick Merrick
Page 20, Allied Bank
Nick Merrick
Page 21, Wilshire Associates
Jaime Ardiles-Arce
Page 23, Wilshire Associates
Jaime Ardiles-Arce
Page 24, Gensler Santa Monica
Nick Merrick
Page 25, Micronomics
Chas McGrath
Page 26, Epson America, Inc.
Marco Lorenzetti
Page 26, Jeppesen
Jon Miller, Hedrich Blessing
Page 27, Jeppesen
Jon Miller
Page 27, Union Bank of Switzerland
Jaime Ardiles-Arce
Page 28, Morrison & Foerster
Marco Lorenzetti
Page 28, Perkins Coie
Peter Aaron
Page 29, Chevron Corporation
Chas McGrath
Page 29, Davis Polk & Wardwell
Nick Merrick